THE
NO-COOK
COOKBOOK

THE
NO-COOK
COOKBOOK

*100 easy & delicious
recipes that don't
need an oven*

SHARON HEARNE-SMITH

Quercus

CONTENTS

Foreword   7
Introduction   9
Your No-cook Pantry   12
Useful Kit   14
No-cook Menu Ideas   16

BREAKFAST & BRUNCH   18
SNACKS & CANAPÉS   48
SOUPS   76
SALADS   96
VEGETARIAN DISHES   112
FISH DISHES   146
MEAT DISHES   172
DESSERTS   194

Index   218
About the Author   224

FOREWORD

Whether you are an avid home cook or a total beginner who doesn't even know how to switch on the microwave, the genius of 'no-cook' recipes is that with just a few ingredients and very little equipment you can create wonder in the kitchen. This book will provide confidence to those who don't know how to cook and inspiration to those who do.

After the success of Sharon's first book, *No-bake Baking*, it's no surprise that her follow-up, *The No-cook Cookbook*, is filled with fun and achievable recipes, all created with a generous sprinkling of her trademark retro charm, and made simple with thorough and meticulous instructions that demystify even the most complicated of techniques.

Using just a few basic kitchen tools, Sharon has sliced, stirred, folded, grated and blended up a collection of wild and wonderful recipes that are bound to excite home cooks! As you flip through the beautiful pages you will no doubt wonder how on earth she has managed to create such stunning dishes without even turning on the oven. Get ready to find out…

Donal Skehan
Food writer, photographer and presenter

INTRODUCTION

For anyone who's ever said: 'I can't cook', 'I'm too busy', or 'I don't feel like cooking' (which surely covers most of us!), this book shows you how to put delicious food on your table in a totally new way. You'll discover how to transform fresh ingredients into vibrant and nutritious meals with absolutely no need for an oven, hob or microwave, instead using a range of simple methods, clever twists and smart kitchen shortcuts to get easy and impressive results.

Following on from my previous book, *No-bake Baking* (which is packed full of tempting oven-free cakes and treats), this book goes a step further and shows how every meal of the day can be rustled up without conventional cooking, giving 100 simple and inspiring recipes for breakfast, lunch and dinner, as well as snacks and party food, plus some more sweet treats thrown in for good measure. You really don't have to be an accomplished cook – or even have a kitchen, for that matter! – to make these dishes. Armed with fresh ingredients, some basic tools and a few shop-bought conveniences, this is a flexible and foolproof approach that anyone can master. The only concession to heat is the use of the kettle and toaster on occasion. So if you can make yourself a cup of tea and some toast then you're off to a great start.

My 'no-cook' philosophy is about far more than just assembly and involves simple methods to get the best out of your ingredients, such as marinating items like mushrooms and courgettes, curing fish and meat, and soaking dry goods like shiitake mushrooms, noodles, bulghur wheat and couscous. The recipes are all based on ingredients or concepts that would usually be cooked, offering fun no-cook takes on classics like ravioli, risotto, burgers, falafel, pizza, lasagne, quiche, hollandaise sauce, and even a 'hot' pot, as well as innovative new ideas including fruit sushi, a smoked salmon crêpe cake and doughnuts with a difference. While lots of my recipes are very quick to make, those which do take longer also give tips for preparing in advance in stages. All are sure to hit the spot, whether you're feeding grown-ups or kids, and regardless of skill level or experience.

Nowadays, it's all too easy to succumb to ready meals, but they can be soulless and lack the love that homemade meals dish up in doses, not to mention the joy that comes from preparing food yourself. Having said that, I'm not averse to using a few good 'cheat' ingredients within a recipe. An ever-increasing range of items can be bought ready-to-use from supermarkets, such as toasted nuts and seeds, roasted peppers, frozen prepared veg, cooked peeled prawns, pouches of pre-cooked pulses and grains, and ready-baked pastry cases (check out more recommendations on pages 12-13). Such ingredients could of course be prepared from scratch at home, but given that their shop-bought counterparts usually taste just as good (if not better) and are much more convenient, they offer a brilliant way to save yourself time and sometimes even money, while still putting homemade food on your plate. Furthermore, shortcuts like these also help take the worry out of cooking. No more burned nuts, or soggy overdone rice. In fact, this goes for the whole no-cook approach, since when there's no cooker involved there's no risk of pans bubbling over, and no fear of opening the oven door to find a cremated roast.

Besides being easy and accessible, the majority of this food is also very healthy, since none of the recipes involve frying in oil or basting in butter, but instead rely on fresh ingredients, simply prepared and assembled, and in many cases kept raw, thereby retaining all their natural nutrients and antioxidants. While I'm by no means claiming all my recipes would suit the official 'raw food' diet, many are a nod to that style of eating, though with more straightforward methods and ingredients. There are also lots of vegetarian and gluten-free options labelled throughout the book, while other recipes include simple tips for adapting to suit these diets.

Believe it or not, there are yet more bonus benefits to be had from this book: it follows that no-cook recipes are perfect for keeping the heat out of the kitchen if living or holidaying in a hot climate, not to mention saving on power too. And since most of the methods need only a handful of basic kitchen utensils and the occasional small appliance (see useful kit on page 14) you can get stuck in just about anywhere you go, from the tiniest holiday-let kitchen to a caravan or even in the office. So whether you're looking for fresh new ideas, easy weeknight food, meals to prepare with kids, or you're taking tentative first steps into the kitchen, these delicious, innovative, no-cook recipes are sure to inspire and excite.

Sharon

YOUR NO-COOK PANTRY

Many recipes in this book get clever with convenience products, helping you 'cheat' your way to a delicious meal by making the most of pre-cooked or ready-to-use ingredients. Often these handy items cost little more than the same raw produce cooked from scratch, and taste just as good (if not better!), while also saving lots of time and even taking the stress out of cooking – no more crying over burned or ruined food. Here are the main convenience items you'll find used throughout the book; generally available in supermarkets, they are super to keep stocked in your pantry ready to use in no-cook recipes or simply to make life easier.

GRAINS, PULSES & NOODLES
Cans of chickpeas, cannellini, haricot and black beans
Pouches of cooked basmati, white long-grain or wholegrain rice
Pouches of cooked red, white or mixed quinoa
Pouches or cans of lentils
Pre-cooked egg noodles – fresh from the chiller cabinet

VEGETABLES
Artichoke hearts
Canned or frozen sweetcorn
Cooked beetroot – vacuum-packed from the fruit and veg aisle; choose the type that's not in vinegar
Frozen spinach – pre-cooked and ready to use once defrosted
Frozen peas

Ready-mashed potato
Roasted red peppers – often in jars with brine, usually in large pieces, though chopped roasted mixed peppers in oil are also available and can be substituted where appropriate
Sundried tomatoes – ones in oil are nicest

MEAT
Cooked beef and spiced beef slices
Cooked chicken pieces
Cooked chorizo
Cooked crispy streaky bacon strips (smoked/unsmoked)
Cooked duck from a roast crispy half duck available pre-packed in the supermarket or even ordered from your local takeaway (and thus served warm)
Cooked pulled pork

Cooked turkey slices

Cooked smoked/unsmoked ham – buy pre-packed or request slices from the deli counter

Cooked black pudding – from the deli counter

Parma, Serrano or other cured hams

Pastrami

Smoked duck and chicken

FISH

Cooked clams – in jars with brine

Cooked mussels – available with or without shells

Cooked prawns – peeled or in their shell; available fresh and frozen

Cooked white crab meat

Pre-cooked seafood mix – often comes in a dressing or marinade, which is fine to include; available fresh and frozen

Smoked mackerel fillets

Smoked and hot-smoked salmon or trout

STORE CUPBOARD

Balsamic glaze – found next to oils and vinegars

Bruschetta

Cocktail blinis – often sold next to fish or fresh dips

Crispy onions – in the dry foods aisle of supermarkets

Crispbreads and French or Melba toasts

Crostini

Croutons

Dried rice paper sheets – available in various sizes from Asian stores

Instant dashi – a convenient powdered Japanese stock, available from Asian stores

Pickled eggs

Pickled ginger

Pickled quails' eggs – sometimes found in supermarkets, particularly at Christmas, or try delis and specialist food stores

Pickled onions

Stock cubes, powder or concentrate – beef, chicken, fish or vegetable

Salted popcorn

Vegetable crisps

NUTS & SEEDS

Cooked chestnuts – available in cans, jars and pouches throughout the year though more abundant at Christmas

Dukkah – an Egyptian blend of toasted nuts, seeds, herbs and spices, typically used as a dip; available in most supermarkets and Middle Eastern stores

Granola

Roasted hazelnuts

Roasted nut and seed mix

Toasted coconut flakes

Toasted flaked almonds

Toasted pine nuts

Toasted sesame seeds – sold in some supermarkets or easy to buy online; the untoasted variety isn't quite as flavoursome, but fine to use if easier to find

SWEET

Amaretti biscuits

Continental sponge flan case

Mini pastry cases

Pancakes or crêpes

Shortbread biscuits

USEFUL KIT

Step away from your cooker! The recipes in this book take the oven, hob and microwave out of the equation and instead show you how to get fast and impressive results using little more than your kettle, toaster, fridge-freezer and a few other kitchen tools. Below are the key pieces of equipment that feature instead of a cooker, with some helpful notes to bear in mind. Where a particular item is required for a recipe, you'll find it specified after the list of ingredients. If you don't have all of these items, don't worry – there are often simple alternatives, while many of the recipes need no special equipment at all. Although not listed, don't forget that you'll also need basics like crockery, cutlery, utensils, measuring jugs and scales, plus extras like baking paper and cling film.

Food processor / jug blender / mini blender
Sometimes these three appliances are interchangeable as they essentially chop and blend, but they do all have slightly different functions and are best suited to different jobs. While a food processor can be used to blend soups and sauces, a jug blender gives a much smoother finish and the new wave of high-speed jug blenders ensures an amazingly smooth finish in just seconds.

Unless your food processor has a smaller bowl insert, a sauce like the hollandaise (page 42) is best made in a jug blender because of the small volume. Since the melted butter needs to be poured in while the machine is blending, a mini blender (which usually has a completely sealed top) isn't suitable in this case.

Although it will take somewhat longer, a good old-fashioned knife will often take the place of a food processor or mini blender. Be sure it is nice and sharp, and that you slice as thinly or chop as finely as necessary. Meanwhile, if you need to crush ingredients into crumbs, a resealable food bag and rolling pin can work very well.

Electric mixer / whisk
If you need an alternative to this, you can always use a simple hand whisk. It will take much longer, but with a bit of patience you will eventually achieve just as good a result.

Pestle and mortar
If you don't have one of these to hand, there are a few simple alternatives. Depending on what the ingredients are, either chop them finely with a sharp knife, or place them on a chopping board and crush under a heavy-based pan. Another option is to use a coffee grinder.

Spiraliser / mandolin / julienne peeler
Spiralisers and mandolins are top of kitchen-gadget wishlists right now, but if you don't have either of these, you can in fact use a julienne peeler or a simple vegetable peeler to create similar results. While it may take a little longer and the resulting vegetables shapes won't be entirely the same, it is possible to achieve long thin strips once you get the technique right. In fact, even a long, sharp knife will do the trick with a bit of work. It's also now possible to buy packets of spiralised fresh vegetables from some supermarkets.

NO-COOK MENU IDEAS

Whatever the meal or occasion, this book is bursting with recipe ideas to help you put together the perfect menu, with the no-cook element bound to be a fun talking point with family and friends. Since so many of the dishes can be prepared ahead, you can get organised well in advance and keep your cool when it's time to serve. Here are some example menus to kick-start your imagination.

THE KIDS WILL LOVE:
Banana, oat & pecan mini muffins (page 23)

Fun fruit sushi (page 29)

Fresh apple 'doughnuts' (page 32)

Chia pudding pops with coconut, raspberry & banana (page 36)

Pizza skewers (page 180)

Striped smoothie jelly (page 214)

PACK UP A PICNIC:
Speckled scotch eggs with black pudding & hollandaise (page 42)

Meat 'loaf' with olive salsa (page 183)

Gazpacho (page 94)

Three-cheese cocktail quiches (page 72)

Beetroot pâté allotment pots (page 70)

Exotic fruit cups (page 196)

PARTY TIME:
Chicken 'koftas' with peanut dip (page 56)

Blue cheese & bacon truffle pops (page 59)

Mexican beef tartare with spicy avocado sauce (page 66)

Beetroot & bean sliders (page 137)

DIY sushi cones (page 151)

Pulled pork Asian lettuce cups (page 174)

LUNCH BOX LOVELIES:
Falafel wraps with spinach pesto & pickled red cabbage (page 128)

Vegetable quinoa sushi rolls (page 52)

Hot & sour chicken noodle pots (page 190)

Prawn pad thai (page 169)

Ginger power balls (page 38)

SOPHISTICATED SUPPER:
Lemon & walnut goats' cheese blinis with
blackberries & basil (page 55)
Beetroot, coconut & lemongrass soup (page 92)
Gravadlax salmon (page 159)
Smoky aubergine and pulled pork 'hot' pots
with cucumber salad (page 188)
Greek yoghurt pannacotta with rosewater,
honey & pomegranate (page 207)
Chocolate orange truffles (page 199)

A SUMMER GARDEN PARTY:
Avocado & cucumber soup (page 78)
Vietnamese pulled pork summer rolls (page 62)
Courgette 'pappardelle' with mozzarella
& minted pea pesto (page 127)
Easy-peasy paella (page 156)
Watermelon pizza with fig, feta & raspberry
dressing (page 124)
Mango mousse cake (page 200)

MOVIE NIGHT MUNCHIES:
Sesame prawn toasts (page 50)
Cheesy chilli poppers (page 75)
Crunchy crab & corn cakes with New
Orleans dipping sauce (page 60)
Family-style Mexican layer pot (page 191)
Salted caramel popcorn fudge (page 212)

CHRISTMAS CLASSICS:
Brussels sprout salad with bacon, pecan,
cranberries & maple dressing (page 100)
Herby soft cheese tart with nutty pastry,
grapes & watercress (page 118)
Chunky chicken & duck pots with winter
salad (page 176)
Smoked salmon crêpe cake with watercress
(page 170)
Balsamic cherry fool (page 203)
Sin-free fruit & nut chocolate triangles
(page 204)

BREAKFAST
& BRUNCH

NO-COOK BREAKFAST TOPPINGS

(V) (GF)

whipped espresso butter

Who would believe that something so simple could be so heavenly? This addictive fluffy butter is delicious spread on toast or scones, or dolloped on warm pancakes.

MAKES 275G

225g unsalted butter, softened

1 tsp espresso coffee powder

50g clear honey

ESSENTIAL KIT:

Electric mixer or hand whisk

Beat the softened butter with an electric mixer or by hand with a whisk, until really pale, fluffy and creamy. Beat in the espresso powder and honey until well mixed and smooth. This will keep for a week or two, covered, in the fridge. Allow to soften before serving.

FOR A TWIST...

- Make 'jam butter', by adding 100g of your favourite jam instead of the espresso and honey (makes 325g).

- Use 100g of nut butter or apple or pumpkin purée instead of espresso powder (makes 375g).

blackberry & apple no-cook jam

Embrace the power of super-healthy chia seeds and witness them work their magic as they thicken this delicious fruit mixture into a simple no-cook jam. This recipe requires barely any hands-on preparation, just a bit of fridge time, and is delicious spread on scones or served with yoghurt and granola.

MAKES 400G

250g blackberries

1 apple

25g clear honey

1 tbsp chia seeds

1 tsp ground cinnamon

Place the berries in a medium bowl and crush with a fork, leaving just a bit of texture. Peel the apple and roughly grate it in. Stir in the honey, chia seeds and ground cinnamon until well blended.

Cover and chill in the fridge for 1–2 hours, until thickened. This will keep in the fridge for a few days.

continued overleaf

spiced orange hazelnut butter

You may never buy a shop-bought nut butter again, after trying this quick homemade treat, which can be easily adapted to use any nuts and flavourings you like. Spread it on toast or crumpets, or use for the Fresh Apple Doughnuts (page 32).

MAKES 325G
**300g roasted hazelnuts
(whole or chopped)
2 tbsp sunflower oil or
light olive oil
2 tsp mixed spice
2 tsp vanilla extract
¼ tsp sea salt flakes
Finely grated zest of
1 orange**

ESSENTIAL KIT:
Food processor

Blitz the nuts in a food processor for 1 minute until finely chopped. Add the oil, mixed spice, vanilla extract, salt and orange zest. Blitz again for 2–3 minutes, scraping down the sides occasionally, until you have a smooth, thick and creamy nut butter.

Store in an airtight container in the fridge for up to two weeks.

FOR A TWIST...
- Turn this into a delicious chocolate hazelnut spread by stirring 100g of melted dark chocolate (at least 70% cocoa solids) and 2 teaspoons of cocoa powder through the finished nut butter. In this case, you can either keep or omit the orange zest as you prefer.

cinnamon mascarpone

Dollop this creamy deliciousness on warm pancakes or waffles (a crispy bacon slice also goes nicely here) or serve with poached fruits like pears, apricots or plums, use as a cake filling or simply devour from the spoon.

MAKES ABOUT 275G
**250g mascarpone
2 tbsp maple syrup
2 tsp ground cinnamon**

Place the mascarpone in a medium bowl and stir to loosen. Add the maple syrup and cinnamon and mix everything together until well blended. Serve at once or keep covered in the fridge for up to a few days.

BANANA, OAT & PECAN MINI MUFFINS

(V) (GF)

With no baking and only five ingredients, these little gems (shown in the photo on page 20) are super-quick and easy to make – and even have a similar texture to their baked counterpart. Keep them nice and healthy by using sugar-free jam if possible, in any flavour you like. Kids will love making these, not to mention eating them – they're great little on-the-go snacks. If you want larger muffins, just double all the quantities and set in six regular-sized paper cases.

MAKES 12

1 banana
100g rolled oats (choose gluten-free oats if necessary)
2 tbsp sugar-free apricot jam
1 tsp ground cinnamon
50g pecan nuts
Your choice of jam, topping or spread, to serve (see pages 21–22 for no-cook varieties)

ESSENTIAL KIT:
12 mini paper muffin cases
12-hole mini muffin tin
Mini-blender (or sharp knife)

Pop the paper cases into the muffin tin and set aside.

Peel the banana and break it into chunks in a medium bowl. Mash with a fork until smooth. Add the oats, jam and cinnamon. Blitz the pecans in a mini-blender until very finely chopped, or chop them as finely as possible with a sharp knife, and add. Stir everything together until well mixed.

Divide the mix evenly between the paper cases. Press the mixture down well, levelling the tops with the back of a spoon. Cover and chill in the fridge for at least 1 hour, until firm.

These will last for a couple of days, covered, in the fridge. Enjoy as they are or serve with your favourite jam, topping or spread.

FOR A TWIST...

• Use your favourite nut butter instead of the apricot jam.

• Make a nut-free (and even more nutritious) version, using 50g of wheatgerm instead of the ground pecan nuts.

CASHEW & FIG BREAKFAST BARS

(V) (GF)

Nutty, chewy and sweet, these moreish no-cook wonderbars require just a handful of simple ingredients, and are healthier than most bars and flapjacks since they contain only natural fruit sugar. They're fast to make and will keep for ages, though don't top with the figs until you're ready to eat. To make them even more delicious, serve with a dollop of the lemon ricotta yoghurt on page 26 or the coconut and passion fruit dip from page 29.

MAKES 8 BARS (OR 16 SQUARES)

Sunflower oil, for greasing
250g pitted Medjool dates
200g cashew nuts
100g rolled oats (choose gluten-free oats if necessary)
Finely grated zest of 1 large orange
4 fresh figs

ESSENTIAL KIT:

17.5cm square cake tin or baking dish
Food processor

Grease the tin with oil, line with non-stick baking paper and set aside.

Place the dates, nuts, oats and orange zest into a food processor. Blitz everything until it forms a smooth, slightly sticky ball. Using damp hands or the back of a spoon, spread the mixture out evenly in the tin. Cover and chill in the fridge for 2 hours or overnight, until firm.

Once set, remove from the tin. Cut the slab into four strips and then cut each strip in half across to give 8 rectangular bars (or in half again to give 16 squares). These will keep in the fridge, layered between baking paper in an airtight container, for up to two weeks.

When ready to serve, trim the figs and cut each one into six slices. Arrange three fig slices on top of each bar, overlapping to fit if necessary. Enjoy straight away or wrap in individual baking paper parcels if eating on the go.

FOR A TWIST...
- Use peeled kiwifruit instead of figs. Or use two kiwifruit and two figs for a more colourful finish.

SPEEDY POPPY SEED 'PANCAKES'

with lemon ricotta yoghurt

(V) (GF)

These clever little pancakes involve no cooking but just a bit of time to set in the fridge, so you can make them the night before and enjoy a fuss-free morning. It's a fun and healthy recipe for kids to help with, especially as there are no hot pans involved. Make sure to shape the mixture into cakes immediately after blending, or it can become quite crumbly and dry to handle. Milled flaxseed is simply another name for ground linseed, and can be found in most supermarkets or health food stores. If you have a choice, use the golden variety rather than the darker brown option. They result in a prettier pancake, but it's not the end of the world if you can't find them.

SERVES 4

300g milled flaxseed
2 tbsp poppy seeds
1 tsp ground cinnamon
Pinch of salt
2 tbsp coconut oil
125ml maple syrup
Seeds from ½ vanilla pod
      or ½ tsp vanilla extract
      or vanilla bean paste

LEMON RICOTTA
      YOGHURT:

250g ricotta
100g natural yoghurt
Seeds from ½ vanilla pod
      or ½ tsp vanilla extract
      or vanilla bean paste
75g lemon curd

TO SERVE:

125g blueberries
½ tsp poppy seeds

Line a tray with non-stick baking paper and set aside.

To make the 'pancakes', toss the flaxseed, poppy seeds, cinnamon and salt together in a large bowl. Add the coconut oil and massage it through until well blended. Make a well in the centre and pour in the maple syrup along with 50ml of water. Add the vanilla seeds, extract or bean paste. Stir everything together to give a crumbly mixture that binds when squeezed together.

Shape the mixture into 12 patties, 8cm wide (about 40g each), and arrange them on the prepared tray as you go. Cover and chill in the fridge for at least 2 hours or overnight, until firm. These will keep, covered in the fridge, for up to a week.

When ready to serve, spoon the ricotta and yoghurt into a medium bowl and whisk until smooth. Add the vanilla seeds, extract or bean paste. Then ripple two-thirds of the lemon curd through the mixture.

Arrange three pancakes in a stack on each serving plate and dollop a spoonful of the ricotta yoghurt on top, followed by a dollop of the remaining lemon curd. Scatter with blueberries (either halved or whole) and decorate with poppy seeds. Serve with the remaining ricotta yoghurt in a small bowl on the side.

FOR A TWIST...

- Shape the pancake mixture into about 24 balls, which can be kept in the fridge for a healthy 'grab and go' treat.

FUN FRUIT SUSHI
with coconut & passion fruit dip

(V) (GF)

Fruit 'sushi' is a novel breakfast idea to brighten up your morning, as well as a great way to introduce kids (and adults!) to the concept of sushi if they haven't tried it before. For an extra nod to the real thing, you can even use strips of nori seaweed instead of the lime zest. If you prefer, use shop-bought coconut yoghurt in the dip, but in that case leave out the desiccated coconut and also the honey, as the yoghurt will likely already contain sugar.

MAKES 12

1 lime (optional)
1 x 250g pouch of cooked basmati rice
3 medium strawberries
¼ small mango
½ thumb-sized piece of fresh ginger, peeled and finely grated
1 tbsp clear honey
Seeds from ½ vanilla pod or ½ tsp vanilla bean paste

COCONUT DIP:

100g natural yoghurt
1 tbsp desiccated coconut
1 tsp clear honey
1 passion fruit

ESSENTIAL KIT:

Kettle
Mini-blender

Half-fill the kettle with water and put it on to boil. Line a large tray with kitchen paper and another with non-stick baking paper and set aside.

Using a vegetable peeler, peel a long strip of zest from all around the centre of the lime, if using. Trim the strip down to 8cm in length and then thinly slice this into 12 long strips. Place in a small bowl, cover and set aside. These give the sushi an authentic look, but are not necessarily for eating, so omit if you prefer.

Transfer the rice to a small bowl and pour over enough just-boiled water to cover. Cover and set aside for 5 minutes.

Meanwhile, prepare the fruit. Trim the strawberries and very thinly slice from top to bottom. You need 12 slices, not counting the ends (cook's treat). Lay them in a single layer on the tray lined with kitchen paper and press another piece of kitchen paper lightly on top. This removes excess moisture from them.

Peel the wedge of mango and cut the flesh into 12 thin slices. Trim down to 2cm x 5cm rectangles (more sneaky offcuts for the cook!). Arrange in a single layer on the same tray and top with another piece of kitchen paper.

Put the grated ginger in a small bowl and stir in the honey. Carefully peel the fruit slices off the kitchen paper and arrange in a single layer on the tray lined with baking paper. Brush the ginger honey over each one and leave to marinate and soften, while you prepare the rest.

continued overleaf

Drain the rice well and, while still warm, blitz it in a mini-blender until finely chopped. It should stick together easily when squeezed. Scoop it into a medium bowl and stir in the vanilla seeds or bean paste. Using damp hands, shape the rice into 12 even-sized oval balls (about 20g each). Arrange on a serving platter as you go. Cover and chill in the fridge until ready to serve. These can be made up to two days ahead.

To make the dip, stir together the yoghurt, coconut and honey in a small bowl. Scoop out the passion fruit pulp and ripple it through the yoghurt. Spoon into a small dipping bowl and keep covered in the fridge until ready to serve.

When ready to serve, top six rice balls with three slightly overlapping slices of strawberry each. Top the remaining six rice balls with two slightly overlapping slices of mango each. If using the lime zest, place one strip across the centre of each ball, curving down the sides. Add the bowl of passion fruit dip to the platter and serve.

Alternatively, serve in single portions, with three sushi (for four people) or six sushi (for two people) on each serving plate, with a separate dipping bowl for each one.

FOR A TWIST...
- Top with alternative fruits, like pineapple, papaya or melon.

PEACH MELBA SMOOTHIE BOWL

(V)

A smoothie bowl is a healthy and fun alternative to cereal or even dessert. The mixture should be thicker than a regular 'drinking' smoothie, and almost scoopable. This classic peach and raspberry flavour combination is just as delicious here as in the original dessert. Have all your ingredients ready to go and whizz up just before you want to serve. Milled flaxseed is another name for ground linseed, and is available in many supermarkets and health food stores.

SERVES 2
150g frozen raspberries
50g natural yoghurt
2 tsp clear honey
1 tbsp milled flaxseed
Juice of ½ lime
**Thumb-sized piece of fresh
    ginger, peeled and
    roughly chopped**
3 peaches
25ml orange juice
1 tbsp wheatgerm

TOPPINGS:
2 tbsp granola
**2 tbsp toasted coconut
    shavings**
**Small handful of fresh
    (organic, unsprayed)
    edible flowers (optional)**
1 peach

ESSENTIAL KIT:
**2 x 175ml ice cream
    coupe-style glass
    bowls (about 10cm
    in diameter), chilled**
Jug blender

To prepare the raspberry smoothie, place the raspberries in a blender with the yoghurt, honey, flaxseed and lime juice. Blitz the mixture until as smooth as possible. Divide it evenly between the serving bowls and chill in the fridge.

Rinse out the blender jug ready to prepare the peach smoothie. Put the ginger in the blender. Halve, de-stone and roughly chop the peaches, and add them to the blender, along with the orange juice and wheatgerm. Give everything a good whizz until the mixture is as smooth as possible.

Spoon the peach smoothie over the top of the raspberry smoothie. If you like, you can insert a long spoon or skewer down to the bottom of the bowl and drag the raspberry smoothie up the inside of the glass to create a nice marbled pattern as it mixes with the peach smoothie.

Sprinkle the granola over the top of each bowl, followed by the coconut shavings and edible flowers, if using. Halve the remaining peach, discard the stone and cut each half into six slices. Place the slices side by side, pointing from the edge of each bowl into the centre so they look like sun-rays. Serve straight away.

FRESH APPLE 'DOUGHNUTS'

(V) (GF)

Okay, so these are not real doughnuts, but you will be pleasantly surprised by how delicious (and addictive) they are, not to mention fun to make and far healthier than their sugary namesakes. Kids especially will love making and eating these – so why not turn it into a fun party game and see who can be the most creative with their toppings and decoration? These are great for breakfast, or as a healthy snack at any time of day.

MAKES 12

300g full-fat cream cheese

100g peanut, almond or cashew nut butter

2 tbsp fruit purée or coulis

1 tsp maple syrup or clear honey

2 large apples, either red or green or 1 of each

3 tbsp chocolate spread or toffee sauce (optional)

75g mixture of your chosen toppings (see below)

TOPPINGS:

Dried fruit, e.g. golden raisins, cranberries, dried apricots or goji berries

Nuts, e.g. hazelnuts, pecans, almonds or pistachios

Seeds, e.g. pumpkin, sunflower, toasted sesame seeds or linseed

Roasted nut and seed mix

Toasted coconut flakes

Bee pollen

Edible flowers

ESSENTIAL KIT:

Apple corer

Line a tray with non-stick baking paper and set aside.

Divide the cream cheese evenly between two small bowls. Mix the nut butter into one and the fruit purée or coulis into the other. Stir ½ teaspoon of maple syrup or honey into each bowl. Cover and set aside until ready to use. This can be made up to one day in advance.

Use the apple corer to remove the core of each apple. Cut each apple into six even-sized slices (including the ends) and lay them flat on the prepared tray (with the ends cut side up).

Spread the nutty cream cheese over six of the slices and the fruity cream cheese over the other six, leaving the centre hole clear. Now, for the really fun bit. Use your selection of toppings to decorate the apple doughnuts as you like. You can also chop your toppings into smaller pieces if you prefer. Either arrange them on top of the apple slices or press the creamy side down onto the toppings to stick.

As a further flourish, drizzle chocolate spread or toffee sauce over the apple doughnuts, if you like. To loosen the sauce for drizzling, spoon it into a small bowl and sit the bowl in another bowl of just-boiled water. Leave for a minute or two until the edges start to melt and give it a good stir. Leave in the heat until a drizzling consistency is achieved.

These can be made up to one day ahead and kept covered in the fridge. Serve on a tiered cake stand or layered between small squares of baking paper in a nice box.

FOR A TWIST...

- Use chocolate spread instead of nut butter, or jam instead of fruit purée.

- Sprinkle the tops with cake sprinkles, for a treat!

'CARROT-CAKE' OVERNIGHT OATS

Also known as bircher muesli, oats soaked overnight in milk make for a delicious porridge that doesn't involve any labouring over the stove. Traditionally, bircher muesli is flavoured with apple, but this version uses ingredients you would usually expect in a carrot cake, so it might almost fool you into believing you are getting away with eating cake for breakfast!

SERVES 2

Finely grated zest and juice of ½ orange
25g sultanas or raisins
100g rolled oats
2 tbsp wheatgerm
1 tbsp desiccated coconut
½ tsp mixed spice
Good pinch of freshly grated nutmeg plus extra to serve (optional)
1 small carrot, peeled and finely grated
300ml whole milk or unsweetened almond milk
1 tbsp maple syrup

TOPPING:

50g full-fat cream cheese
25g natural or vanilla yoghurt
6 pecans or walnuts

Pour the orange juice into a small bowl. Add the sultanas or raisins, stir them to coat and leave aside to soak.

Place the oats in a medium bowl and add the wheatgerm, coconut, mixed spice and nutmeg. Stir together and make a well in the centre.

Reserve a small handful of the grated carrot for serving, keeping it covered in the fridge. Drop the rest into the dry ingredients with the reserved orange zest.

Pour the milk, maple syrup and soaked sultanas or raisins (and any remaining orange juice) into the centre. Stir everything together until well mixed. Cover and chill in the fridge for at least 8 hours or overnight.

Spoon the cream cheese into a small bowl and give it a good beat to loosen. Add the yoghurt and stir through until smooth. Cover and chill in the fridge until ready to serve.

Once ready, give the porridge a stir and divide between serving bowls. Dollop the cream-cheese mixture on top, scatter with the reserved grated carrot and crumble over the pecans or walnuts. Grate a little more nutmeg on top if you like and serve.

FOR A TWIST...

- Make a beetroot and chocolate version, using 75g grated beetroot (raw or from a vacuum pack) instead of the carrot and adding a tablespoon of cocoa or raw cacao powder to the mix as well.

CHIA PUDDING POPS
with coconut, raspberry & banana

(V) (GF)

Chia pudding has become a very popular healthy breakfast option. This recipe, which uses coconut milk as its base, can also be served as a regular chia pudding if set in glasses (though omit the banana in this case, unless eating immediately). However, freezing the mixture turns the pudding into fun and good-for-you ice pops. The kids won't believe their luck when you offer them a lolly for breakfast!

MAKES 8

1 x 400ml can coconut milk
50g chia seeds
Finely grated zest and
**   juice of 1 lime**
2–3 tsp honey
125g raspberries
2 bananas

ESSENTIAL KIT:

Mini-blender (or bowl and
**   fork)**
8 x 75ml ice-pop moulds
8 wooden lolly sticks
**   (unless sticks come**
**   with your mould set)**

Pour the coconut milk into a large jug and add the chia seeds and lime zest and juice. Give the mixture a good stir until evenly blended and then add enough honey to give your preferred sweetness. Leave aside for about 30 minutes to thicken slightly.

Meanwhile, blitz the raspberries in a mini-blender until you have a smooth purée. Alternatively, crush them in a bowl with a fork until as smooth as possible.

When ready to make the pops, peel and cut each banana into 16 even-sized slices.

To assemble, spoon a teaspoonful of the raspberry purée into the bottom of each pop mould. Spoon in about 30g of the thickened chia mixture. Slide a slice of banana down each side of each mould, to squish into the chia pudding mixture. Repeat the layers one more time until the moulds are full and all ingredients have been used up. Insert the stick into the centre of each pop and place level in the freezer for at least 8 hours or overnight, until frozen.

When ready to serve, place the pop mould in hot water for a few seconds to release the pop and enjoy!

FOR A TWIST...

- Make 16 smaller pops as a breakfast canapé (or kiddie treat).

GINGER POWER BALLS

(V)

Great as snacks on the run or a sin-free treat, these power balls of goodness are crammed with health-giving ingredients: fresh ginger aids digestion, molasses is full of iron and wheatgerm is a bountiful source of energy, fibre, protein and vitamins, while linseed and chia seeds are packed full of omega-3. As for goji berries, with a superfood like that where do we even start? If you can't find toasted sesame seeds, just use regular ones.

MAKES 20

Thumb-sized piece of fresh ginger, peeled and roughly chopped
250g pitted Medjool dates
100g almonds
1 tbsp chia seeds
1 tbsp linseeds
1 tbsp wheatgerm
1 tsp blackstrap molasses
Good pinch of sea salt (optional)
50g rolled oats

COATINGS:

1 tbsp shelled pistachios, finely chopped
2 tbsp goji berries, roughly chopped
1 tbsp toasted sesame seeds
1 tsp cocoa or raw cacao powder

ESSENTIAL KIT:
Food processor

Line a tray with non-stick baking paper and set aside.

In a food processor, blitz the ginger, dates, almonds, chia seeds, linseeds, wheatgerm, molasses and sea salt (if using), until the mixture is smooth and sticky.

Put the mixture into a medium bowl and add the oats. Mix together until well combined. Using damp hands, shape the mixture into 20 even-sized balls (just over 20g each), arranging them on the tray as you go.

To coat the balls, tip the pistachios, goji berries, sesame seeds and cocoa powder into separate small bowls. One at a time, roll five balls in each coating, tossing them about until evenly coated, and return them to the tray as you go. These can be enjoyed straight away. Alternatively, they will keep in the fridge, layered between pieces of baking paper in an airtight container, for up to a week.

FOR A TWIST...

• Make bars instead of balls, by spreading the mixture into a lined 17.5cm square cake tin using the back of a damp spatula or spoon. Mix together the prepared coatings (except the cocoa), scatter evenly over the top and press down gently to stick. Chill in the fridge for 1 hour to set, before cutting into 8 rectangular bars or 16 smaller squares.

BLT SALAD
with avocado aioli

Tasty yet healthy, this salad makes a lovely breakfast or brunch and looks so cute served in lettuce-leaf bowls. The avocado aioli is a great alternative to regular egg-based aioli; it keeps for much longer and is suitable for anyone with an egg intolerance. Spread it on sandwiches, use as a dip or simply devour from the bowl. Instead of croutons, you could crumble Melba toast, bruschetta or crispbread on top.

SERVES 4

1 head cos lettuce
½ small red onion, peeled
    and finely sliced
175g vine-ripened cherry
    tomatoes, halved
8 strips of cooked crispy
    streaky bacon (smoked
    or unsmoked)
25g croutons
Sea salt and freshly ground
    black pepper

AVOCADO AIOLI:

2 ripe avocados
1 tsp Dijon mustard
Good pinch of cayenne
    pepper
Juice of 1 lemon
1 large garlic clove, peeled
    and roughly chopped
50ml extra virgin olive oil
Small handful of fresh
    chives, finely chopped

ESSENTIAL KIT:

Food processor or blender

To make the aioli, scoop the avocado flesh into a food processor or blender. Add the mustard, cayenne, lemon juice and garlic. Give everything a good blitz until smooth. With the motor running, pour in the olive oil to give a smooth, thick mixture. Spoon into a small bowl and stir through the chopped chives. Season to taste. This can be made up to two days in advance and kept covered in the fridge.

Trim the cos lettuce and arrange a large, crisp and unbroken leaf as a 'bowl' on each serving plate. You may need to trim the underside spine of the cos leaves a little, in order for them to sit up straight and work as a bowl.

Shred the remaining leaves and pop into a large bowl. Add the red onion and tomatoes. Spoon half of the aioli over and give everything a gentle toss until evenly coated.

Pile spoonfuls of the dressed salad into each of the cos lettuce bowls. Arrange two of the bacon strips on top of each, scatter with croutons and serve with the remaining avocado aioli on the side.

FOR A TWIST...

- For canapé-sized servings, use Little Gem lettuce leaves instead of cos.
- Sprinkle with finely sliced fresh red chilli for a fiery kick.

SMOKED MACKEREL KEDGEREE

This kedgeree can be prepared a day in advance, making it a perfect, no-fuss breakfast or brunch for any day of the week. It also works just as well for dinner or in a lunch box instead, if that's what you fancy. Look for packets of crispy fried onions in supermarkets.

SERVES 4

2 x 250g pouches of cooked white long grain or wholegrain rice
2 tbsp olive oil
Juice of 1 lemon
1 tsp turmeric
1 tsp ground coriander
1 tsp ground cumin
4 smoked mackerel fillets
Large handful of fresh coriander leaves
4 spring onions, finely sliced
150g frozen spinach, thawed
2 pickled eggs
4 tsp crispy onions
Sea salt and freshly ground black pepper

DRESSING:

75g mayonnaise
75g natural yoghurt
1 tsp mild, medium or hot curry powder
Juice of ¼ lemon

ESSENTIAL KIT:

Kettle

Half-fill the kettle with water and put it on to boil.

To make the dressing, place the mayonnaise, yoghurt, curry powder and lemon juice in a small bowl. Stir everything together until well blended. Cover and chill in the fridge until ready to serve. This can be made up to two days in advance.

Place the rice in a medium bowl and pour over enough just-boiled water to cover. Cover and set aside for 5 minutes.

To make the kedgeree, pour the oil and lemon juice into a large bowl. Add the turmeric, ground coriander and cumin and whisk until well blended. Remove the skin and dark residue from the mackerel, flake it into chunks and set aside.

Drain the rice well and add it to the bowl, stirring well until evenly coated. Roughly chop half the coriander and add along with the spring onions. Squeeze the spinach dry and add it to the bowl, along with the mackerel. Toss everything together gently and season to taste (bearing in mind that the mackerel will be salty). This can be made up to one day ahead.

Divide the kedgeree between serving bowls and drizzle with a little of the creamy dressing. Quarter the eggs and nestle two pieces into each bowl of rice. Scatter the crisp onions and remaining coriander leaves on top and give everything a final twist of black pepper. Serve at once with the remaining dressing in a small bowl.

FOR A TWIST...
- Use hot smoked trout or salmon instead of mackerel.
- To make this gluten-free, omit the crispy onions and sprinkle with toasted flaked almonds instead.

SPECKLED SCOTCH EGGS
with black pudding & hollandaise

These cheat's Scotch eggs are so much easier than the real thing, with no greasy deep-frying nor any boiling of eggs (you'll see…). Instead of sausagemeat, the outer layer is actually a chickpea blend. Cooked black pudding, which adds the speckles, is available from many delicatessens and supermarket deli counters. Regular hollandaise sauce can be tricky to make, but once you learn this foolproof no-cook version, you'll never look back.

SERVES 4 FOR BRUNCH

1 x 400g can chickpeas
100g sun-dried tomatoes
    (from a jar)
50g rolled oats
2 tbsp almond butter
Small handful of fresh flat-
    leaf parsley or chives
½ small red onion, peeled
50g cooked black pudding
4 pickled eggs
25g toasted flaked almonds
75g mixed salad leaves
2 tbsp extra virgin olive oil
Juice of ½ lemon
Sea salt and freshly ground
    black pepper

HOLLANDAISE SAUCE:

75g butter, softened
3 egg yolks
¼ tsp Dijon mustard
Pinch of cayenne pepper
Juice of ½ lemon

ESSENTIAL KIT:

Kettle
2 heatproof bowls (1 small
    and 1 medium)
Food processor
Mini-blender or sharp knife
Jug blender

Put the kettle on to boil, about a quarter full.

Start with the hollandaise sauce. Cut the butter into small pieces and place in a small heatproof bowl. Sit this inside a larger heatproof bowl and pour enough just-boiled water between the two to reach halfway up the sides of the small bowl. Leave to melt, stirring occasionally.

For the Scotch eggs, drain and rinse the chickpeas and place in a food processor. Add the sun-dried tomatoes, oats and almond butter. Pick off the parsley leaves or rip the chives into pieces, and add these. Roughly chop the onion and add this too, then blitz to a rough paste. Spoon into a medium bowl and crumble in the black pudding, discarding any skin. Gently stir until evenly mixed but still in pieces. Season to taste.

Divide the mixture into four even-sized portions. Take one and shape it into a flat round, about 1cm thick. Sit an egg in the middle, wrap the mixture around the egg and press the seam together. Make sure it is a nice egg shape. Repeat with the remaining ingredients to make four. These can be made up to two days in advance and kept covered in the fridge.

When the butter is melted, remove from the hot water and leave to cool slightly.

When nearly ready to serve, blitz the almonds in a mini-blender until fairly finely chopped. Alternatively, finely chop them by hand. Place on a plate and then carefully roll each Scotch egg in the almonds, until evenly and lightly coated. (Don't do this too early, or the nuts will start to go soft.)

continued overleaf

To complete the hollandaise, place the egg yolks, mustard, cayenne and lemon juice in a jug blender, and blitz until combined. With the blender running, pour in the melted butter in a slow, steady stream. This will give a smooth sauce of pouring consistency. For a thicker sauce, chill in the fridge for about 1 hour or overnight, until set. If you want to warm it through to serve, pour into a small jug and sit this in a bowl of just-boiled water. Alternatively, just serve it at room temperature.

When ready to serve, place the salad leaves in a large bowl. Drizzle the oil around the inside edge of the bowl, followed by the lemon juice. Season lightly. Gently toss the leaves around the bowl until evenly coated.

Serve the Scotch eggs whole or cut in half. Arrange the dressed leaves to one side. Spoon the hollandaise sauce over the eggs or serve in a small bowl or jug.

FOR A TWIST...

- Make veggie Scotch eggs by replacing the black pudding with the same quantity of cooked lentils or crumbled chestnuts.

- Serve the chickpea mixture as 'meat' balls. Shape the mixture into about 20 balls, and serve with pasta, rice or in a pitta pocket or wrap. Double the almond quantity if coating.

MEXICAN TOSTADAS

with chorizo, avocado & black beans

A perfect hangover cure, packed with flavour and nutrients, plus that all-important chilli kick. The egg yolks are optional and should be avoided for young kids, pregnant women or anyone frail. But don't dismiss them outright, as they are full of nutrients and antioxidants – think of the delicious oozing yolk of a soft-boiled or poached egg, and reconsider.

SERVES 4

1 ripe avocado
½ lime
4 flour tortillas
50g smoked cheese, grated
16 cooked chorizo slices
100g sour cream
4 very fresh egg yolks (optional)
Handful of fresh coriander
1 red chilli, thinly sliced
Sea salt and freshly ground black pepper

TOMATO SALSA:

200g vine-ripened cherry tomatoes
50g sun-dried tomatoes
½ small red onion, peeled
1 small garlic clove, peeled
Handful of fresh coriander
¼ tsp smoked paprika

DRESSED BEANS:

Finely grated zest and juice of ½ lime
1 small garlic clove, peeled
Handful of fresh coriander
1 tbsp olive oil
1 x 400g can black beans

ESSENTIAL KIT:
Toaster

To make the salsa, quarter the cherry tomatoes and cut each piece in half again to give small dice. Put in a medium bowl. Finely chop the sun-dried tomatoes, onion, garlic and fresh coriander leaves, and add to the bowl. Sprinkle in the smoked paprika and give everything a good stir together, then season to taste and set aside.

For the beans, place the lime zest and juice into a medium bowl. Finely chop the garlic and fresh coriander leaves and scatter in. Add the oil and whisk to combine. Season to taste. Drain and rinse the black beans and toss them through the dressing to coat.

Just before serving, quarter the avocado, peel and discard the stone, and slice each quarter thinly. Squeeze the lime juice over to prevent them turning brown.

When ready to serve, fold the tortillas into quarters and pop each one into a toaster. Toast for 1–2 minutes until beginning to colour. Carefully remove, open out into halves and flip back into quarters the opposite way around. Pop back into the toaster for a further 1–2 minutes. The tortillas should be warmed through, lightly coloured and just turning crispy on the edges, but not crisp all over.

To assemble, carefully open up a warmed tortilla on each serving plate. While still warm, sprinkle grated cheese all over each one. Arrange four chorizo slices in a single layer and spoon the tomato salsa on top. Pile some dressed beans on one side and lay the avocado slices on them. Dollop sour cream on one side, with the egg yolk in the middle, if using. Scatter with coriander and red chilli, and serve.

BLOODY MARY BEANS

A heartier twist on the classic morning-after cocktail, these beans have a lovely vodka kick. But if that's too much for you to contemplate first thing in the morning (or of course if you are pregnant, there are kids involved or you don't drink alcohol), then just leave it out and serve up non-alcoholic Virgin Mary beans instead, which are just as delicious.

SERVES 4

2 celery sticks, plus 4 from the heart with leaves
500ml passata
4 tbsp sun-dried tomato paste
2 tbsp olive oil
1 tbsp vodka (optional)
2 x 400g cans cannellini or haricot beans
Splash of Worcester sauce
Splash of hot pepper sauce, such as Tabasco
Juice of ½ lemon
4 crispy streaky bacon strips
8–12 pieces of bruschetta, crispbread or toast
Sea salt or celery salt and freshly ground black pepper

GARNISHES (CHOOSE 3):
2 pickled quail's eggs, halved (or 1 pickled egg, quartered)
4 cornichons
4 cooked peeled prawns
4 radishes
4 green olives
4 pickled chillies

ESSENTIAL KIT:
Food processor
4 x 275ml serving glasses/jars
4 small skewers

Roughly chop the two standard celery sticks, place in a food processor and blitz until finely chopped. Add the passata, sun-dried tomato paste, olive oil and vodka (if using) and blend to combine. Pour into a medium bowl.

Drain and rinse the beans and stir them through the sauce. Then, mix in enough Worcester sauce, hot pepper sauce and lemon juice to taste (and for that classic Bloody Mary flavour). Season with salt or celery salt and pepper to taste. This can be made up to three days in advance, but is best brought back to room temperature before serving.

Divide the bean mixture between the serving glasses or jars and sit each one on a small serving plate. Stand one of the remaining celery sticks, leaf side up, in each one, and insert a strip of bacon alongside it. Slide your choice of three garnishes onto a small skewer, repeating four times. Balance a skewer across the top rim of each glass. Serve with bruschetta, crispbread or toast, and a little dish of celery salt if you like.

FOR A TWIST...

- Make this into a quick and easy main meal, by tossing the Bloody Mary beans with carrot or courgette that has been cut into long spaghetti-like strands with a spiraliser, mandolin or julienne peeler.

- For vegetarians, omit the bacon and prawns, and replace the Worcester sauce with a veggie-friendly variety or with mushroom ketchup or marmite.

SNACKS
& CANAPÉS

SESAME PRAWN TOASTS
with chilli lime sauce

With this quick no-cook version of the takeaway classic, there's no deep-fat fryer in sight! Prawn toasts make great canapés, served with the chilli lime sauce on the side and a spoon for drizzling. Alternatively, serve four per person as a starter with individual bowls of sauce. They would also be an excellent accompaniment to the Avocado & Cucumber Soup (page 78) – but serve without the sauce in that case. Shop-bought French or Melba toasts, or any type of crispbreads, are an ideal cheat ingredient here (the photo shows 4cm x 8cm Melba toasts). If you can't find toasted sesame seeds, just use regular ones.

MAKES 16

**175g cooked, peeled
  prawns**
¼ tsp Chinese five spice
½ tsp light soy sauce
**½ thumb-sized piece of
  fresh ginger, peeled and
  roughly chopped**
**1 small garlic clove, peeled
  and roughly chopped**
Juice of ½ lemon
16 Melba toasts
3 tbsp toasted sesame seeds
**Small handful of fresh
  coriander leaves**

CHILLI LIME SAUCE:

**Finely grated zest and
  juice of 2 limes**
75g chilli jam or sauce
4 tsp fish sauce

ESSENTIAL KIT:

Mini-blender

To make the sauce, place the lime zest and juice into a small bowl, along with the chilli jam and fish sauce, and mix everything together well. This can be made up to three days ahead and kept in the fridge.

Place the prawns, Chinese five spice, soy sauce, ginger, garlic and lemon juice in a mini-blender. Blend everything to give a smooth, thick paste. This can be made up to one day in advance and kept covered in the fridge.

When ready to serve, divide the mixture evenly between the toasts, spreading it right to the edges. Scatter the sesame seeds on a plate and press the prawn side of each toast down on them until evenly coated. These are best assembled no more than an hour before serving or the toasts may begin to soften.

Arrange on a platter or individual serving plates, and garnish with scattered coriander. Serve at once with the chilli lime sauce.

VEGETABLE QUINOA SUSHI ROLLS
with miso dip

(V) (GF)

These colourful little numbers will have vegetarians (and non-veggies alike) reaching for more. Shop-bought cooked quinoa sold in pouches is a handy cheat's ingredient, and works well in place of rice in this sushi, giving a nutty flavour and lovely texture, as well as lots of protein. A bamboo mat is a great investment if you want to master sushi; they're sold cheaply in Asian stores and many supermarkets. If you can't find toasted sesame seeds, regular ones are fine.

MAKES 24

2 x 250g pouches of cooked red, white or mixed quinoa
2 tbsp tahini paste
2 tsp soy sauce or tamari for gluten-free
1 small carrot, peeled
125g cooked beetroot (from vacuum pack, not in vinegar)
½ small yellow pepper, de-seeded
4 nori seaweed sheets
25g baby spinach
25g sprouted peas or salad cress
1 tbsp wasabi paste

MISO DIP:
Juice of 1 lime
½ thumb-sized piece of fresh ginger, peeled
2 tbsp white miso paste
2 tsp clear honey
1 tsp toasted sesame seeds

ESSENTIAL KIT:
Food processor
Mandolin (or julienne peeler or sharp knife)
Bamboo sushi mat

For the dip, pour the lime juice into a screw-cap jar. Finely chop the ginger, and add to the jar along with the miso paste, honey and sesame seeds. Add 2 tablespoons of water, screw the lid on tight and shake until well blended. This can be made up to three days ahead and kept in the fridge.

Place half of the quinoa in a food processor and blitz until coarsely chopped. Add the tahini paste and soy sauce and blitz again briefly to combine. Transfer to a medium bowl and stir in the remaining quinoa until well mixed.

Next, prepare the vegetables. Cut the carrot into long thin shreds with a mandolin, julienne peeler or sharp knife. Cut the beetroot into 1cm-wide sticks. Slice the pepper into thin strips.

Line the sushi mat with a piece of cling film and lay a nori sheet on top, with the shiny side facing down. Spread it with a quarter of the quinoa in an even layer, leaving a 1cm margin along the edge furthest from you. Pile up a quarter of the prepared vegetables, spinach and sprouted peas or cress in a row across the middle.

To roll, lift the edge of the mat (and cling film) closest to you and begin to roll it away from you. Tuck the front edge of the nori inwards as it curls over and then continue to pull the mat away from you to create a complete and tight roll. Dip a finger in water and run it down the seam edge of the seaweed to seal it closed. Repeat with the remaining ingredients to give four rolls. These will keep for a couple of days, covered in the fridge.

continued overleaf

Using a long, sharp knife, trim any ragged ends from the rolls and then cut each one into six pieces and arrange on serving plates, cut-side up. Shake up the dipping sauce, divide between four small bowls and pop one onto each plate. Squeeze a little wasabi paste onto each plate and garnish with coriander.

FOR A TWIST…

- For a more traditional sushi, replace the quinoa with 2 x 250g pouches of cooked rice. The rice will need to be soaked in boiling water, and covered, for 5 minutes. Then drain and blitz briefly in a processor until finely chopped and sticky when squeezed.

- Use any selection of fillings you like: try avocado, beansprouts, courgette, pre-cooked prawns or chicken.

LEMON & WALNUT GOATS' CHEESE BLINIS
with blackberries & basil

Blinis are a great shop-bought base for canapés. Here, they are topped with flavoured goats' cheese, complemented by a blackberry and aromatic basil, a lovely combination of tastes and textures which also looks quite beautiful. Blinis are best warmed through and then allowed to cool, rather than served straight from the fridge, so it is worth doing this in advance and then only adding the toppings at the last minute.

MAKES 12

200g rindless, soft goats' cheese (at room temperature)
50g walnuts, finely chopped
25g hard cheese (Parmesan or vegetarian equivalent), finely grated
Finely grated zest and juice of ½ lemon
12 cocktail blinis
12 blackberries
12 small basil leaves
Sea salt and freshly ground black pepper

ESSENTIAL KIT:

Piping bag fitted with plain 1cm nozzle or disposable piping bag cut to this size opening
Toaster

Beat the goats' cheese in a medium bowl to loosen it up. Add the walnuts, Parmesan, lemon zest and juice, and mix everything together until well blended. Season to taste.

Spoon the mixture into the prepared piping bag and chill in the fridge until ready to serve. This can be made up to one day in advance. Remove from the fridge about 15 minutes before use to soften a little for piping.

When ready to serve, lay the blinis out in a single layer on top of the toaster. You may need to work in batches. Turn the toaster on to heat as usual. Leave the blinis to warm through for 2–3 minutes, until softened slightly and warm, using tongs to turn them over halfway through. Be careful not to allow the blinis to fall in or it may be tricky to get them out again. Once warmed, remove the blinis to a serving platter and leave to cool.

Once the blinis are cool, pipe an even amount of the goats' cheese mixture on each one (about 20g), in a spiral pattern from the middle. Alternatively, dot the mixture in a pretty pattern all over the top. Sit a blackberry, pointed side up, in the centre of each one. Garnish with a basil leaf and serve.

FOR A TWIST…
- Instead of a blackberry, top with a piece of fresh fig, pear, apple or a grape.

CHICKEN 'KOFTAS'
with peanut dipping sauce

These moreish bites combine the traditional shape of Indian koftas with South-east Asian flavours. Quick and easy to make, they can be prepared in advance for perfect stress-free party food. Use the lemongrass trimmings for an infused tea, or to flavour soup, curry or rice.

MAKES 20

400g cooked chicken

2.5cm piece of fresh ginger, peeled and chopped

1 red chilli, chopped, and de-seeded if you prefer

50g smooth peanut butter

Large handful of fresh coriander leaves, plus extra to serve

50g salted peanuts, finely chopped

Sea salt and freshly ground black pepper

PEANUT DIP:

100g smooth peanut butter

75ml coconut milk

2 tsp light soy sauce (tamari for gluten-free)

2 tsp fish sauce

1 tsp sriracha or other hot chilli sauce (optional)

Juice of 1 lime

5cm piece of fresh ginger, peeled and chopped

1 garlic clove, peeled and roughly chopped

ESSENTIAL KIT:

Food processor

10 lemongrass sticks or wooden ice lolly sticks

Mini-blender or jug blender

Line a tray with non-stick baking paper and set aside.

Tear or chop the chicken into rough pieces and place in a food processor. Add the ginger, chilli, peanut butter and coriander leaves. Blitz to a smooth paste. The mixture should stick together when squeezed. Season to taste.

Shape the chicken mixture into 20 sausage shapes about 2.5cm wide and 5cm long (about 25g each). Arrange them on the prepared tray as you go. If using lemongrass for the sticks, trim each one down to about 8cm long, leaving the root intact, then slice in half lengthways. Push the top end of the trimmed lemongrass or lolly stick into the centre of each kofta, like a lollipop. Cover and chill in the fridge for at least 30 minutes or overnight, until firm. These can be made up to two days ahead.

To make the dipping sauce, place all the ingredients into a blender and blitz until as smooth as possible. Pour into a small bowl, cover and chill in the fridge until needed. This can be made up to three days in advance. It is best removed from the fridge about 20 minutes before serving, so it can reach room temperature and soften.

When ready to serve, place the chopped peanuts in a small serving bowl. Arrange the chicken koftas on a serving platter, with the bowls of peanut dipping sauce and chopped peanuts beside. Garnish with scattered coriander leaves, and serve. To eat, dip a kofta first into the sauce, then into the nuts.

FOR A TWIST...

- Turn into a main meal by tossing the peanut sauce through cooked noodles. Serve with the koftas (sticks optional), and scatter the coriander and chopped peanuts on top.

- Shape the chicken mixture into balls or patties and serve in pitta pockets or on burger buns with the peanut dip and salad.

BLUE CHEESE & BACON TRUFFLE POPS

These savoury pops are really quick and simple to make but are sure to impress your guests, espcially when they reach the fruity surprise hidden in the centre. Choose a slightly sweet, not too salty blue cheese that isn't excessively soft or crumbly. If you want these to be gluten-free but can't find suitable pretzels, you can use lolly sticks instead.

MAKES 12

25g crispy cooked streaky bacon (unsmoked)

150g creamy blue cheese

12 small grapes, red or green or a mix of both

12 pretzel sticks (gluten-free if necessary, or lolly sticks)

Plum, fig or pear chutney, to serve (optional)

ESSENTIAL KIT:

Mini-blender

Line a small plate or tray with non-stick baking paper and set aside.

Blitz the bacon in a mini-blender until finely ground. Tip into a small bowl and set aside.

Remove any rind from the cheese and divide the cheese into 12 even-sized pieces. Flatten out one piece into a small disc in your hand, about 5cm across and 5mm thick. Place a grape in the centre and then work the cheese around it to enclose it fully and make a neat ball. Roll it in the bacon crumbs until evenly coated. Repeat to make 12, arranging them on the tray as you go.

Cover and chill in the fridge for at least 1 hour or overnight, until firm. These can be made up to two days in advance.

When ready to serve, carefully insert a pretzel stick into the centre of each cheese truffle, right into the grape. Arrange the pops, stick pointing up, on a long platter. Spoon the chutney (if using) into a small bowl and place on the platter to serve.

FOR A TWIST…

- To make these vegetarian, replace the bacon crumb with finely chopped pecan nuts or vegetable crisps. If using the crisps, then coat just before serving so they retain their crunch.

- Use a piece of dried apricot or a dried cranberry in the centre, instead of a grape.

CRUNCHY CRAB & CORN CAKES
with New Orleans dipping sauce

Crab and corn cakes are an American classic, set off with this spicy New Orleans sauce. Although these ones are not conventionally cooked, the polenta coating provides a satisfying crunch. Serve them at parties, for lunch or as a tasty snack.

MAKES 30

200g cooked mashed potato

125g sweetcorn kernels (drained or defrosted weight)

1 tbsp sweet or hot chilli sauce

200g white crab meat

2 spring onions, finely chopped

Large handful of fresh coriander leaves

50g fine polenta or cornmeal

Sea salt and freshly ground black pepper

DIPPING SAUCE:

125g mayonnaise

1 tbsp capers

1 tbsp prepared horseradish sauce

1 tbsp sweet or hot chilli sauce

2 tsp Dijon mustard

½ tsp paprika

½ tsp Cajun seasoning

Juice of ½ lemon

1 small garlic clove, peeled and roughly chopped

ESSENTIAL KIT:

Mini-blender

Line a tray with non-stick baking paper and set aside.

First, make the dipping sauce. Place all the ingredients in a mini-blender, and blitz until smooth and creamy. Then season to taste. Transfer to a small serving bowl, cover and set aside in the fridge. This can be made up to one week in advance.

To make the crab cakes, place the mash in a medium bowl and add the sweetcorn and chilli sauce. Squeeze the crab meat until as dry as possible and add to the mix, along with the spring onions. Reserve a few coriander leaves for garnishing, then finely chop the rest. Add them to the mixture and stir everything together until well blended. Season to taste.

Shape into 30 small patties (about 15g each), arranging them on the tray as you go. Tip the polenta into a wide, shallow bowl and carefully roll a crab cake in it until evenly coated all over. Repeat for all 30. Cover and chill in the fridge for at least 1 hour or overnight, to firm up a little. These can be made up to one day ahead and kept covered in the fridge.

Place the dipping sauce bowl in the centre of a serving platter and arrange the crab cakes around. These are best kept in the fridge until just before serving. Garnish with scattered coriander, and serve immediately.

DOLMA ROLLS
with fennel & feta dip

(V) (GF)

Dolma rolls consist of vine leaves wrapped around a delicious rice filling. Vine leaves are widely available in jars from Middle Eastern, Asian or speciality food stores. Alternatively, use chard leaves, softened briefly in just-boiled water. For an extra kick, serve with pickled chillies, if you like. The dip works as a filling for pittas or flatbreads, or alongside chicken.

MAKES 12

1 x 250g pouch of cooked long grain/basmati rice
50g dried apricots, chopped
25g sultanas
Finely grated zest and juice of ½ lemon
1 small garlic clove, crushed
1 small red-skinned apple
2 spring onions, sliced
Large handful of flat-leaf parsley, chopped, plus extra leaves to serve
½ tsp ground cinnamon
12 vine leaves
Seeds from ½ pomegranate
1 tbsp toasted pine nuts

FENNEL & FETA DIP:

1 tsp fennel seeds
200g feta cheese
1 spring onion, chopped
Large handful of fresh flat-leaf parsley leaves
100ml olive oil
Juice of ½ lemon
Sea salt and freshly ground black pepper

ESSENTIAL KIT:

Pestle and mortar
Mini-blender
Kettle

For the dip, very finely grind the fennel seeds with a pestle and mortar. Tip into a mini-blender, add the feta, spring onion, parsley, olive oil and lemon juice, and blitz until smooth and pale green. Season with a little pepper and spoon into a bowl. This can be made up to two days ahead and kept covered in the fridge.

Half-fill the kettle with water and put it on to boil. Place the rice in a medium bowl. Add the apricots, sultanas, lemon zest and garlic and toss everything together. Pour over enough just-boiled water to cover. Cover and set aside for 5 minutes.

Meanwhile, core and quarter the apple, grate the flesh into a large bowl, then add the lemon juice. Toss to coat, to prevent discolouring. Add the spring onions, parsley and cinnamon.

Drain the now softened rice and dried fruits and add them to the apple. Mix everything together well and season to taste.

Rinse the vine leaves well in cold water and dab them dry with kitchen paper. Lay them out on a clean work surface, vein side up (shiny side down). Trim and discard any stems.

Place about 2 tablespoons of rice mixture near the stem of each leaf. Fold in the left and right sides of each leaf over the filling. Then fold the stem end over the filling and continue to roll into a tight cylinder. These can be served straight away, or made up to one day in advance and kept covered in the fridge. They are best eaten at room temperature.

When ready to serve, arrange the dolmas on a large platter with the dip. Scatter the pomegranate seeds on top, along with the pine nuts and parsley. Serve at once.

FOR A TWIST...
- For an extra kick, use 1 or 2 tablespoons of traditional Greek ouzo (or sambuca) instead of fennel seeds in the dip.

VIETNAMESE PULLED PORK SUMMER ROLLS

These delicious fresh rolls make great party food and are much healthier than their pastry-based spring-roll cousins. With their translucent wrappers and one end left open, you get a beautiful glimpse at what's inside, and can drizzle the sauce into them before eating. Kids will love these, and can help with assembling them. One fun option is to arrange all the ingredients on a large platter in the centre of the table so everyone can build their own.

MAKES 10

100ml rice wine vinegar
2 tsp caster sugar
½ cucumber
50g glass or rice noodles
150g cooked pulled pork
1 medium carrot, peeled
2 spring onions, sliced
1 small red chilli, finely sliced, de-seeded if you prefer (optional)
Small handful each of fresh mint and coriander
Small handful of fresh Thai basil (optional)
100g beansprouts
10 x dried rice paper sheets (22cm round)

DIPPING SAUCE:

Thumb-sized piece of fresh ginger, peeled
1 small red chilli, finely sliced, de-seeded if you prefer (optional)
2 tbsp fish sauce (check for gluten)
2 tsp clear honey
Juice of ½ lime

turn for more →

Fill the kettle with water and put it on to boil. Line a tray with non-stick baking paper.

Place the vinegar and sugar in a small resealable food bag and shake until the sugar dissolves. Using a mandolin or vegetable peeler, shave the cucumber into thin ribbons. Add them to the liquid in the bag and leave to pickle for about 10 minutes, tossing occasionally.

Meanwhile, make the dipping sauce. Shred the ginger into thin matchsticks. Place it into a screw-cap jar, along with the sliced chilli (if using), fish sauce, honey, lime juice and 4 tablespoons of water. Screw the lid on tightly and give it a good shake. This can be made up to three days in advance and kept in the fridge.

Lay the noodles in a wide dish and pour over enough just-boiled water to cover. Cover and leave to soak for 4–5 minutes for glass noodles, or 8–10 minutes for rice noodles (or according to the packet instructions), until tender, stirring halfway through.

Then continue preparing the filling ingredients. Tear or chop the pork into small pieces if necessary. Cut the carrot into matchsticks using a mandolin, julienne peeler or sharp knife. Make sure all the other ingredients are prepared and ready.

Once tender, drain the noodles and rinse them in cold water. Also drain the cucumber.

To assemble the rolls, pour a few centimetres of warm water into a bowl wide enough to take a rice paper sheet. Pop one sheet in to soak for 10–15 seconds until soft and pliable. Being careful not to tear it or stick it to itself, lift it out of the water and lay it out flat on a clean tea towel. Arrange a small amount of each prepared ingredient on top, including the beansprouts

continued overleaf

ESSENTIAL KIT:

Kettle

**Mandolin, julienne/
  vegetable peeler or
  sharp knife**

but not the coriander, layering them up in a straight line down the middle, stopping about 5cm from the edge closest to you. The rolls look nice when some ingredients poke out of the end, so don't worry if anything overhangs the top edge of the rice paper. Now pick up the edge closest to you and fold it up onto the filling. Fold in the left side of the rice paper over the filling and continue to roll from this direction to give a neat roll.

Repeat to make 10 in total, arranging them spaced apart on the tray as you go. They can be quite sticky, so don't let them touch. These can be made up to two days ahead, depending on the freshness of your fillings. Layer them between non-stick baking paper if packing away in a container and store in the fridge.

When ready to serve, arrange on a platter and scatter with the coriander. Shake up the sauce, pour it into a small dipping bowl and serve on the side.

FOR A TWIST...

- Use any other fillings that take your fancy. Choose a good mix of colours, textures and flavours, as well as thinking about what's in season. Instead of pork, use cooked chicken, duck, beef, turkey, prawns or salmon, or keep them vegetarian.

- For a speedier, less fishy dip, serve with a shop-bought sweet chilli sauce.

- Omit the pork to keep them vegetarian.

WALNUT-STUFFED CHICORY CUPS

with artichoke & feta purée

(V) (GF)

These classy morsels make great starters or party canapés. The walnut stuffing – sometimes known as 'nut meat' – is full of flavour and also works nicely as a filling for vegetarian tacos. The artichoke and feta purée is equally delicious as a dip or spread. If you can't get chicory, Baby Gem lettuce leaves work just as well.

MAKES 12

75g walnuts

50g sun-dried tomatoes (from a jar)

50g pitted black olives

¼ tsp cayenne pepper

15g vegetarian hard cheese or Parmesan, finely grated

12 chicory leaves (your choice of red or white)

Small handful of fresh basil leaves

Sea salt and freshly ground black pepper

ARTICHOKE PURÉE:

200g artichoke hearts (from a jar)

100g feta cheese

3 tbsp olive oil

Small handful of fresh basil leaves

1 small garlic clove, peeled and roughly chopped

Juice of ½ lemon

ESSENTIAL KIT:

Mini-blender

First make the artichoke and feta purée. Place the artichokes in a mini-blender, crumble in the feta and add the oil, basil leaves, garlic and lemon juice. Blend until smooth. Season to taste (remembering the feta may be salty enough). Set aside. This can be made up to two days in advance and kept in the fridge.

To make the walnut stuffing, first rinse out the mini-blender. Place the walnuts, sun-dried tomatoes, olives and cayenne in the blender and blitz until roughly chopped. Carefully remove the blade from the blender and stir in the cheese. Season to taste. This can be made up to three days ahead and kept in the fridge.

When ready to serve, arrange the chicory leaves on a large serving platter. Spoon the artichoke purée into each one and sprinkle the walnut stuffing mixture on top. Garnish with basil leaves, and serve.

MEXICAN BEEF TARTARE

with spicy avocado sauce

GF

It's important to use super-fresh steak for this recipe as the meat is cured rather than cooked. Since it gets finely chopped, ask the butcher for the end cuts of the fillet, which tend to be cheaper than centre-cut steaks. Chill the steak well in the freezer to make it easier to finely dice. Scooping out the lime shells is a bit of a fiddly job but is worth it if you want to impress guests. However, if you have no patience (and no kids or bored teenagers to put to work), then you can simply spoon the tartare onto the nachos and top with the avocado sauce.

MAKES 10

200g beef fillet steak
1 small garlic clove, peeled and crushed
4 limes
¼ small red onion, peeled and very finely diced
Large handful of fresh coriander leaves
1 tbsp sriracha or other hot chilli sauce
1 tbsp tomato purée
30 mini nachos
Sea salt and freshly ground black pepper

AVOCADO SAUCE:

1 avocado
1 tbsp mayonnaise
⅛ tsp ground cumin
⅛ tsp cayenne pepper, plus extra for dusting
1 lime

ESSENTIAL KIT:

Mini-blender

Using a sharp knife, cut the fillet steak into 5mm dice and pop it into a medium non-metallic bowl or resealable food bag, along with the garlic. Squeeze the juice from the limes over the meat and reserve the lime halves. Toss the meat in the juice until well coated, cover or seal and chill in the fridge for at least 4 hours or overnight, to marinate and cure the meat. Give it a gentle stir (or squidge if in the bag) every so often.

To make the avocado sauce, scoop the avocado flesh into a mini-blender and add the mayonnaise, cumin and cayenne. Squeeze in the juice from the lime, again reserving the lime halves. Blitz until really smooth and season to taste. This can be made up to one day ahead and kept covered in the fridge.

Using a teaspoon, remove and discard any remaining flesh from the reserved lime halves. This will take a bit of fiddly scraping, so allow time. It's worth it!

When ready to serve, drain any excess lime juice that hasn't been absorbed by the meat, then add the diced onion to the bowl or bag. Set aside 10 coriander leaves, then finely chop the remainder and add to the mix. In a small bowl, stir the chilli sauce and tomato purée together until well blended. Add to the meat and gently stir the whole lot together until well mixed. Season to taste.

Sit the prepared lime shells cut-side up on a serving platter, trimming the bases a little if necessary to stop them rocking. Divide the meat tartare evenly between the shells. Stick a nacho upright in each one. Dot a little avocado sauce on top and garnish with the reserved coriander leaves. Dust with a little cayenne pepper. Spoon the remaining avocado sauce into a small bowl and the remaining nachos into another and serve alongside, so people can help themselves.

RETRO SMOKED SALMON MOUSSE
in cucumber cups

GF

These delicious canapés offer the classic combination of smoked salmon and cucumber. The piped mousse and radish 'flowers' give them a retro feel, as if they've just stepped out of one of your granny's cookbooks. They can also be served as a starter, or the salmon mousse makes an excellent dip or spread for crispbreads or toast.

MAKES 14

100g hot-smoked salmon
100g full-fat cream cheese
Finely grated zest and
juice of ½ lemon
1½ tsp finely chopped fresh
tarragon leaves or dill
1 cucumber
7 small radishes
Sea salt and freshly ground
black pepper

ESSENTIAL KIT:

Mini-blender
Piping bag fitted with large
star nozzle (open star
with 7 points, each
about 8mm long)
30mm melon baller (or
small measuring spoon
or teaspoon)

Break the salmon into pieces into a mini-blender, discarding any skin, bones or dark residue as you go. Add the cream cheese, lemon zest and tarragon or dill, and blitz until as smooth as possible. Add enough lemon juice to just taste (taking care not to add too much or you will loosen the mixture), then season. Scoop into the prepared piping bag and set aside on a plate in the fridge, while you prepare the cucumber and radishes. This can be made up to one day in advance.

Peel the cucumber and cut it into 14 circular chunks (each about 2cm long). Using a melon baller, small measuring spoon or teaspoon, scoop out the centre of each piece, leaving the bottom intact and walls about 5mm thick. Arrange them, cavity side up, on a serving platter.

Using a sharp knife, very finely slice the radishes (you need 70 slices) and keep covered until ready to serve.

Pipe a rosette of salmon mousse into each of the cucumber cups (using about 15g per cup). To make the radish roses, roll up one slice to resemble the centre bud of a flower. Then wrap four more slices around the bud to resemble petals. Push the rose into one of the salmon peaks to secure in place and then repeat for all of them. Cover (but not directly touching the tops) and chill in the fridge until needed. These can be assembled up to a few hours before serving.

BEETROOT PÂTÉ ALLOTMENT POTS

(V) (GF)

These cute little pâté pots, designed to look like mini vegetable gardens, with beetroot 'earth', hazelnut 'soil', dill 'grass', and vegetable crudités 'growing' up out of them, are lovely to serve at parties and great fun for kids to help make, and to eat. Choose any selection of crudités you fancy, such as baby carrots (scrubbed and halved lengthways); fine green beans and/or asparagus spears; radishes; sticks of cucumber, celery, courgette or sweet pepper of any colour; cherry tomatoes; chicory leaves; or small florets of broccoli or cauliflower. The beetroot pâté is also delicious spread on crispbreads.

MAKES 8

**300g cooked beetroot
    (from vacuum pack,
    not in vinegar)**
75g full-fat cream cheese
100g feta cheese
2 tsp horseradish sauce
1 tsp clear honey
Grated zest of ½ lemon
25g roasted hazelnuts
Small handful of fresh dill
**Sea salt and freshly ground
    black pepper**
**Crudités, to serve (see
    introduction above)**

ESSENTIAL KIT:

**Food processor or jug
    blender**
8 x 100ml glasses or pots

To make the pâté, place the beetroot in a processor or blender and add the cream cheese, feta, horseradish, honey and lemon zest. Blitz until smooth and season to taste. This can be made up to three days in advance and kept covered in the fridge.

Spoon the pâté into the glasses, glass jars or pots. Chop the hazelnuts finely and scatter a layer of them on top, then finely chop the dill and sprinkle with this too.

Arrange a selection of vegetable crudités sticking out of the beetroot pâté. If using round vegetables like radishes or cherry tomatoes, cut a little slit in each one and perch it on the top edge of the glass. These can be assembled up to one day ahead and kept covered in the fridge until ready to serve.

THREE-CHEESE COCKTAIL QUICHES

(V)

Ready-made mini pastry cases are available in supermarkets or speciality food stores and come in a good variety of flavours and interesting shapes, making them a great no-cook shortcut. Be sure to stir the sun-dried tomatoes into the mixture last, and as lightly as possible, or they tend to squish and discolour the cheese.

MAKES 12

75g ricotta
75g mascarpone
25g hard cheese (Parmesan or vegetarian equivalent), finely grated
Good pinch of freshly grated nutmeg
Large handful of fresh basil leaves
25g sun-dried tomatoes (from a jar), finely chopped
12 mini pastry cases
2 tbsp toasted pine nuts
Sea salt and freshly ground black pepper

Mix the ricotta and mascarpone together in a medium bowl until well blended. Add the Parmesan and nutmeg. Reserving 12 small basil leaves, finely chop the rest and add. Stir everything together until well mixed. Finally, add the sun-dried tomatoes and stir very lightly into the mixture. Season to taste. This mix can be made up to two days ahead and kept covered in the fridge.

Arrange the pastry cases on a serving platter. Divide the filling evenly between the cases (about 15g per quiche). Arrange the pine nuts and one of the reserved basil leaves on top of each one to decorate, add a twist of pepper and serve. These are best assembled no sooner than a few hours before serving so that the cases don't soften.

FOR A TWIST...

- For a non-vegetarian version, ruffle up a small piece of Parma ham or smoked salmon on top of each quiche – pop it on after the nuts but before the basil.

- Top each quiche with a black or green olive half.

PINK GRAPEFRUIT-CURED SCALLOPS

(GF)

This recipe is inspired by Peruvian ceviche, a dish of citrus-cured seafood which has recently become very popular. The scallops are not cooked in the usual sense of the word but are cured by the grapefruit and lime juice; you will be pleasantly surprised by how zingy and delicious they are. Be sure to use extremely fresh scallops and keep them well chilled. Once this recipe wins you over, be sure to try the 'Seared' Tuna Steak on page 148 as well, which is prepared in a similar way. These scallops look especially pretty served on seashells, which you can pick up in homeware stores or from a beach, though make sure to sterilise them before use. Alternatively, serve on nice spoons or tiny saucers.

MAKES 12

1 pink or red grapefruit
Juice of 2 limes
¼ tsp clear honey
¼ tsp fine sea salt
¼ thumb-sized piece of fresh ginger, peeled and finely chopped
½ red chilli, finely chopped, de-seeded if you prefer less heat (optional)
6 very fresh scallops, without roe
Drizzle of extra virgin olive oil
Small handful of fresh coriander leaves
Small handful of fresh mint leaves

ESSENTIAL KIT:

12 scallop shells or other sea shells (see introduction above)

Using a small, sharp knife, cut the peel off the grapefruit. Then, holding it over a small, non-metallic bowl to catch the juice, remove six of the largest segments from between the membranes. Squeeze all the juice from the rest of the grapefruit into the bowl as well. Split the reserved segments in half down their length, and set aside, in a separate bowl.

Pour the lime juice into the grapefruit juice. Add the honey and salt and stir until dissolved. Finally, add the chopped ginger and chilli, if using, and stir.

Slice each scallop in half horizontally to give two discs and slide them into the grapefruit and lime marinade, ensuring they are all submerged. Cover and chill in the fridge for at least 1 hour but up to a maximum of 4 hours. Any longer and the scallops will become tough. If making ahead, have everything prepared ready to simply add the scallops 1–4 hours before serving.

Place a piece of scallop and a piece of the reserved grapefruit in each shell. Spoon the marinade over the top and drizzle with oil. Garnish with scattered coriander and mint leaves. Enjoy the scallops straight away.

FOR A TWIST…
• Use blood oranges instead of the grapefruit, when in season.

CHEESY CHILLI POPPERS

with red chimichurri sauce

These stuffed chillies are not for the faint hearted! Those who dare will love the explosion of flavours and heat. Simple to assemble, they are great fun served as party food with cold beers. Ideally use chillies about 10cm in length, which come in jars of brine from Asian, Mediterranean or Middle Eastern stores, delis or specialist food shops.

MAKES 30–35

200g full-fat cream cheese (at room temperature)
Finely grated zest and juice of 1 lime
50g Cheddar cheese, finely grated
50g toasted, flaked almonds
Large handful of fresh coriander leaves
30–35 pickled chillies (from a large jar)
10–12 Parma or Serrano ham slices (optional)

CHIMICHURRI:

100g roasted red peppers (from a jar)
2 tsp red wine vinegar
½ tsp ground cumin
½ tsp ground coriander
½ tsp smoked paprika
1 garlic clove, peeled and roughly chopped
1 vine-ripened tomato
Sea salt and freshly ground black pepper

ESSENTIAL KIT:

Mini- or jug blender
Piping bag fitted with plain 1cm nozzle, or disposable bag cut to this size opening

First, make the chimichurri. Place the roasted peppers in a blender, with the vinegar, cumin, coriander, paprika and garlic. Blitz until smooth and pour into a medium serving bowl. Quarter the tomato and discard the seedy insides. Finely chop the flesh and stir it through the sauce. Season to taste, then cover and chill in the fridge until ready to serve. This can be made up to three days ahead.

For the filling, spoon the cream cheese into a medium bowl and add the lime zest and juice. Beat together well to loosen the cheese. Add the Cheddar. Finely chop about a third of the almonds and half the coriander leaves and add both. Give the mixture a good stir, until well blended. Season to taste and spoon it into the prepared piping bag.

Drain the chillies well, dabbing them dry with kitchen paper if necessary. Slit one side of each chilli open, right down the length, so you can see inside (but without cutting through to the other side). Discard the seeds. Pipe the cream cheese mixture down the length of each one to fill the cavity.

If using Parma or Serrano ham cut the slices lengthways into three even-sized strips and wrap one piece around each chilli popper. Arrange on a large platter as you go. These can be made up to two days ahead and kept covered in the fridge.

To serve, nestle the bowl of chimichurri sauce on the serving platter with the chilli poppers. Scatter the remaining flaked almonds and coriander over the chillies, and serve.

Alternatively, if serving as a starter, arrange several chilli poppers on each serving plate. Drizzle the sauce over the top and scatter with flaked almonds and coriander.

SOUPS

AVOCADO & CUCUMBER SOUP

(V) (GF)

This elegant soup is quick and easy to make. Serve it chilled, for a refreshing light lunch on a summer's day. The texture of blended avocado gives the soup its creamy consistency and distinctive flavour. Rub a little lemon juice over the cut sides of the reserved avocado to prevent it from discolouring.

SERVES 4

2 avocados

1 cucumber

¼ red onion, peeled and roughly chopped

300ml buttermilk

Juice of ½ lemon

1 tbsp extra virgin olive oil

Small handful of fresh mint leaves

Sea salt and freshly ground black pepper

ESSENTIAL KIT:

Food processor or jug blender

Reserve a quarter of one avocado and of the cucumber. Roughly chop the rest (discarding the skin and stone of the avocados) and place in a food processor or blender. Add the red onion, buttermilk and lemon juice. Blitz everything until really smooth. Season to taste. This can be served at room temperature, or if you prefer, pour it into a large jug, cover and chill in the fridge for at least 1 hour or overnight. The soup can be made up to two days in advance.

When ready to serve, very finely chop the reserved cucumber and avocado. Ladle the soup into serving bowls and scatter the cucumber and avocado on top. Drizzle with olive oil, scatter with mint leaves and serve.

FOR A TWIST…

- Garnish with 1 teaspoon of crab meat or ½ teaspoon of roasted seed mix sprinkled on top of each one.

- Offer this as a refreshing party shot. Divide the quantities in half to make 20 shots. Serve in cucumber 'shot glasses', made by trimming 5 extra cucumbers and cutting them into quarters. Use a small teaspoon to scoop out a hollow down the middle of each piece of cucumber, leaving a 5mm border around the sides and at the bottom of the hole.

SIMPLE ASIAN MISO SOUP

(V) (GF)

This is a classic miso soup recipe, but with the addition of nori seaweed pieces as a twist. Miso is a fermented soybean paste used to enhance flavour. It is rich in nutrients and has health benefits including anti-ageing properties. Dashi is a Japanese stock found in Asian stores and it also comes in a convenient 'instant' powder form. Choose a brand that is MSG-free, and if you're a vegan or vegetarian it's worth reading the label to check the ingredients, as dashi is traditionally prepared with bonito flakes (made from fish) but some brands don't contain fish. You can use vegetable or fish stock instead, if you prefer. Mirin is a sweet rice wine easily found in most supermarkets or Asian stores.

SERVES 4

1 nori seaweed sheet
25g instant dashi
2 tbsp white or red miso paste (check for gluten-free)
1 tbsp mirin
1 tsp light soy sauce (or tamari for gluten-free)
200g silken or firm tofu, drained and cut into 1cm cubes
3 spring onions, finely sliced

ESSENTIAL KIT:
Kettle

Fill the kettle with water and put it on to boil.

Using scissors, cut the nori seaweed sheet into quarters and place the pieces on top of each other. Cut the pile into four strips and then each set of strips into 3–4 bite-sized rectangular pieces. Set aside somewhere safe, where they will not get wet.

Place the dashi in a large bowl and add 800ml of just-boiled water, stirring until dissolved.

Spoon the miso into a small bowl, pour a ladleful of the dashi stock on top and whisk until blended. Then pour this mixture back into the main bowl of stock. This helps prevents lumps.

Stir the mirin and soy sauce thoroughly into the stock. Then add the tofu, spring onions and nori pieces.

Ladle into small bowls and serve at once.

FOR A TWIST...
- Use a small handful of chopped chard, cavolo nero or spinach instead of nori.

MINESTRONE VERDE
with parsley pesto

Ⓥ

This fresh green version of the hearty Italian vegetable and pasta soup is a nice alternative to the more familiar tomato-based classic. Be sure to start with your vegetables at room temperature, as they won't blanch properly if fridge-cold. If you can't find filini pasta (short strands) then break up capellini (angel hair) pasta or fine egg noodles into 2cm lengths instead. The pesto can also be served on small toasts or crispbreads alongside the soup.

SERVES 4

100g filini pasta (short strands)
100g fine green beans, trimmed and finely sliced
100g broccoli, in tiny florets
100g frozen peas, defrosted
25g baby spinach
Small handful each of fresh basil and chives
Vegetable stock cube, powder or concentrate (enough for 1 litre stock)
5g vegetarian hard cheese
2 tsp extra virgin olive oil
Sea salt and freshly ground black pepper
Crusty bread, to serve

PARSLEY PESTO:
1 small garlic clove, peeled
Small handful of fresh flat-leaf parsley leaves
2 tsp toasted pine nuts
1 tbsp extra virgin olive oil
5g vegetarian hard cheese

ESSENTIAL KIT:
Kettle
Mini-blender

Fill the kettle with water and put it on to boil.

To make the pesto, roughly chop the garlic and place in a mini-blender with the parsley and pine nuts. Blitz until roughly chopped. Add the olive oil and blitz again to give a rough pesto. Remove the blade and finely grate in the Parmesan. Mix well, then set aside until ready to serve.

Place the pasta in a small bowl and pour over enough just-boiled water to reach about an inch above. Cover the bowl and set aside for 5 minutes.

Place the green beans, broccoli, peas and spinach in a large bowl. Shred the basil and finely chop the chives, then add both to the bowl. Make the stock up to 1 litre with just-boiled water. Pour it into the bowl, cover and leave for 5 minutes.

Drain the pasta and rinse in boiling water. Stir it in with the vegetables and season to taste.

Ladle the soup into serving bowls and dot with the pesto. Shave the cheese over the top and drizzle with olive oil. Serve at once with crusty bread.

VIETNAMESE BEEF PHO (JUST PHO YOU!)

(GF)

If you've ever visited Vietnam, you will have witnessed stalls heaped with fresh herbs, vegetables and steaming pots of broth and noodles. Pho is one of Vietnam's most loved dishes and, in fact, there it is very popular for breakfast! It's important to chill the beef in the freezer first to make it easier to thinly slice. Because the beef is so thin, it cooks lightly in the heat of the stock. Alternatively, you can use shredded or chopped cooked beef, if you prefer.

SERVES 4

150g beef fillet
Thumb-sized piece of fresh ginger, peeled and sliced
1 garlic clove, peeled and roughly chopped
3 cardamom pods
3 black peppercorns
2 star anise
1 cinnamon stick
200g flat rice noodles
1 lime
Large handful each of fresh coriander, basil (or Thai basil) and mint leaves
4 spring onions, finely sliced
2 red chillies, finely sliced
75g beansprouts
Beef stock cube, powder or concentrate (enough for 1 litre stock)
1 tbsp fish sauce, plus extra to serve
1 tbsp light soy sauce (or tamari for gluten-free), plus extra to serve

ESSENTIAL KIT:
Kettle

Double-wrap the beef in cling film and put in the freezer for 20 minutes to firm up. Fill the kettle and put it on to boil.

Place the ginger and garlic in a small bowl. Crush open the cardamom pods with the side of a knife against a chopping board, and add them to the bowl along with the peppercorns, star anise and cinnamon stick. Pour over 100ml of just-boiled water to submerge. Cover and set aside to infuse for about 15 minutes.

Lay the noodles in a wide dish and pour in enough just-boiled water to submerge. Cover and leave to soak for about 10 minutes (or as per packet instructions) until tender, stirring halfway through. Meanwhile, cut the lime into four wedges and arrange in a large bowl, with the herbs, spring onions and chillies.

When the spice infusion and noodles are both almost ready, put another full kettle on to boil. Using a sharp knife, very thinly slice the beef fillet and set aside.

Place the beansprouts in a small bowl and pour over enough just-boiled water to cover. Leave for 30 seconds to soften a little, then drain them and add them to the garnish bowl.

Make up 900ml of beef stock in a large bowl, using just-boiled water. Strain the reserved spice-infused water through a sieve into the stock, to top it up to 1 litre. If you like, you can add the star anise and cinnamon stick back into the stock for decoration, otherwise discard. Add the fish and soy sauces.

When tender, drain the noodles and divide between four serving bowls. Arrange the beef slices on top. Ladle over the stock and serve at once with the garnish bowl. Serve extra fish sauce and soy sauce on the side.

FOR A TWIST...
- Instead of beef, use prawns, chicken or pork (all ready-cooked). With these, there is no need to firm up in the freezer.

BOUILLABAISSE
with cheat's rouille

GF

Bouillabaisse is a classic French seafood soup, packed full of fish and shellfish, and delicately flavoured with fennel and saffron. It is traditionally garnished with rouille, a spicy sauce thickened with breadcrumbs. This quick, easy, no-cook version makes use of a pre-cooked seafood mix, though don't worry if you can only find one that comes in a dressing or marinade. Pickling the fennel takes a bit of time, but it can be prepared up to a week ahead so it needn't hold you up if you get organised in advance, or you can omit it if you prefer.

SERVES 4

Good pinch of saffron
4 vine-ripened tomatoes, roughly chopped
Fish stock cube, powder or concentrate (enough for 100ml stock)
3 tbsp sun-dried tomato paste
1 small shallot, peeled
1 garlic clove, peeled
1 celery stick
Finely grated zest of ½ orange
Small handful of fresh thyme leaves
1 tsp Dijon mustard
¼ tsp fennel seeds
300g pre-cooked seafood mix (such as prawns, mussels and squid), thawed if frozen
4 large cooked prawns in their shells
Small handful of dill sprigs, to garnish
Sea salt and freshly ground black pepper

turn for more →

Put the kettle on to boil, about a quarter full.

Start by pickling the fennel. Trim the fennel, reserving the fronds. Very finely slice it with a mandolin, food processor or sharp knife. Toss in a colander with the salt and leave to drain over a bowl or sink for about 30 minutes.

Place the saffron for the bouillabaisse in a tiny bowl, pour over 2 tablespoons of just-boiled water and then set aside to steep for 5 minutes.

To make the rouille, using the side of a large knife against a chopping board, crush the garlic and anchovy together until smooth. Place in a small bowl with the mayonnaise, paprika and lemon zest. Season to taste (it may not need salt because of the anchovies). Cover and chill in the fridge until needed. This can be made up to one week in advance.

For the soup, place the tomatoes in a food processor or blender with the saffron and its soaking liquid. Make the stock with 100ml of just-boiled water and add, along with the tomato paste. Roughly chop the shallot, garlic and celery stick, and add to the processor along with the orange zest, thyme, mustard and fennel seeds. Blitz everything together until as smooth as possible. Pour into a large jug and season to taste. Cover and chill in the fridge until ready to use. This can be made up to two days ahead, but is best allowed to come back to room temperature before serving.

continued overleaf

PICKLED FENNEL:

½ small fennel bulb,
    with fronds
1 tsp sea salt
25g caster sugar
25ml rice vinegar

ROUILLE:

1 small garlic clove, peeled
    and roughly chopped
2 anchovy fillets, roughly
    chopped
75g mayonnaise
¼ tsp smoked paprika
Finely grated zest of
    ½ lemon
12 crostini (gluten-free if
    necessary)

ESSENTIAL KIT:

Kettle
Mandolin or food processor
    with slicing blade (or a
    sharp knife)
Food processor or jug
    blender

Returning to the fennel, place the sugar and vinegar in a medium bowl or resealable food bag with 2 tablespoons of water, and whisk or shake until the sugar dissolves. In the colander, rinse the fennel well to remove the salt. Add it to the vinegar solution and push it down until submerged. Cover or seal and chill in the fridge for at least 1 hour or overnight. This can be made up to one week in advance.

Once ready, drain the fennel well and place in a bowl (the same one is fine if you were using a bowl, not a bag). Add the seafood mix and toss together. Ladle the bouillabaisse evenly between serving bowls. Arrange the fennel and seafood mix in a pile in the centre of each one. Sit a whole, cooked prawn on the pile as well. Garnish the soup with the reserved fennel fronds and a few dill sprigs.

Spoon the rouille onto the crostini and serve at once alongside the bouillabaisse.

TUSCAN WHITE BEAN SOUP
with ham & thyme

(GF)

With ingredients that are traditional in many dishes from Italy's Tuscan region, this simple soup is comforting and delicious. Prepare it just before you want to eat, so the stock stays hot. Its chunky texture is robust enough for a main course, especially if served with rustic bread. Be sure to start with your veg at room temperature, as it won't blanch properly if fridge-cold.

SERVES 4

1 small carrot, peeled and roughly grated
1 celery stick, finely sliced
3 spring onions, finely sliced
1 garlic clove, crushed
Small handful of fresh thyme leaves, finely chopped
Big handful of baby spinach
Chicken or vegetable stock cube, powder or concentrate (enough for 600ml stock)
½ tsp Dijon mustard
2 x 400g cans cannellini beans
100g cooked ham, shredded
Large handful of fresh flat-leaf parsley leaves, finely chopped
1 tsp extra virgin olive oil
25g Parmesan, shaved
Sea salt and freshly ground black pepper
Crusty bread (gluten-free if necessary) and salted butter, to serve

ESSENTIAL KIT:
Kettle
Food processor or blender

Fill the kettle with water and put it on to boil.

Place the carrot, celery, spring onions, garlic, thyme and spinach in a large bowl. Make the stock with 600ml of just-boiled water and stir in the mustard. Pour over the vegetables, cover and set aside for 5 minutes.

Drain and rinse the beans and place them in a small bowl. Pour over enough just-boiled water to submerge. Cover and set aside for 5 minutes.

When the beans are ready, scoop a couple of tablespoons of the bean soaking liquid into a food processor or blender and drain the rest from the beans. Tip half of the beans on top of the liquid and blitz until smooth. Stir the bean purée into the vegetables in stock to thicken slightly. Add the remaining whole beans, ham, and all but a little of the chopped parsley, and stir everything together well. Season to taste.

Ladle into serving bowls, and garnish with the remaining parsley. Drizzle with the olive oil, scatter with the Parmesan shavings and serve at once with crusty bread and butter.

FOR A TWIST...
- Make this soup vegetarian, by omitting the ham and using vegetable stock and vegetarian hard cheese instead of Parmesan.
- Instead of spinach, use shredded kale, cabbage or cavolo nero.

THAI RED CURRY MUSSEL BROTH

GF

The sweetness of mussels stands up well to the spiciness of this flavoursome broth. Different curry pastes vary in flavour and heat, so it's best to add the paste gradually, tasting as you go, until you reach a flavour you are happy with. Cooked mussel meat can be bought in packets from supermarkets or some fishmongers, either with or without shells. This soup works best served at room temperature, and if prepared in advance should be removed from the fridge an hour or more before serving, to allow the coconut milk to return to a pouring consistency.

SERVES 4

1 red chilli, de-seeded
1 spring onion
75g sugar snap peas (at
    room temperature)
1 x 400g can coconut milk
4–6 tsp Thai red curry
    paste
2 tsp peanut butter
Thumb-sized piece of fresh
    ginger, peeled and
    roughly chopped
1 small garlic clove, peeled
    and roughly chopped
Large handful of fresh
    coriander leaves
Juice of 1 lime
1 tbsp fish sauce
2 tsp light soy sauce (or
    tamari for gluten-free)
100g cooked mussel meat
Thai spicy crackers, to
    serve

ESSENTIAL KIT:

Kettle
Food processor or
    jug blender

Half-fill the kettle with water and put it on to boil.

Cut the chilli and spring onion into very thin matchsticks and submerge in a small bowl of iced water. Chill in the fridge until ready to serve.

Cut the sugar snaps in half lengthways and place in a small bowl. Pour over enough just-boiled water to cover. Cover and set aside for 4–5 minutes until al dente.

Place the coconut milk, 4 teaspoons of the curry paste and the peanut butter in a food processor or blender. Add the ginger, garlic and two-thirds of the coriander leaves. Pour in the lime juice, fish and soy sauces. Blitz until as smooth as possible. Taste the soup and blitz in the remaining 1 or 2 teaspoons of curry paste for further flavour and chilli punch if you like.

Drain the sugar snaps and rinse well under cold running water until cool.

Ladle the broth into wide serving bowls and arrange the cooked mussels in the centre. Add the sugar snaps around the mussels. Drain the now-curled spring onions and chilli and scatter them over. Scatter the remaining coriander on top and serve with Thai spicy crackers on the side.

FOR A TWIST...
• Use pre-cooked prawns instead of mussels.

CHILLED MELON SOUP
with pickled prawns

This light, refreshing soup is so easy to make. The sharp pickled prawns balance out the sweetness of the fruit. The melon purée is very versatile and can also be used (if the salt is omitted) to serve over ice cream, or as the base for a smoothie. You can even freeze it in lolly moulds or make into a granita by following the freezing and scraping method on page 211.

SERVES 4

1 cantaloupe melon (about 1kg)
½ thumb-sized piece of fresh ginger, peeled and finely grated
Juice of ½ lemon
Extra virgin olive oil, to serve
Small handful of tiny fresh mint sprigs
Sea salt

PICKLED PRAWNS:

Juice of 3 limes
1 tbsp white wine vinegar
½ tsp caster sugar
¼ tsp salt
12 cooked peeled tiger prawns (tails left on if you like)
1 kaffir lime leaf
¼ cucumber

ESSENTIAL KIT:

10mm mini melon baller (or sharp knife)
Food processor or jug blender

To pickle the prawns, pour the lime juice and vinegar into a small, non-metallic bowl or resealable food bag. Add the sugar and salt, then stir or shake until they dissolve. Add the prawns and lime leaf. Peel the cucumber and halve it lengthways. Scoop out and discard the seeds, then slice. Add to the bowl or bag and toss well. Cover or seal and chill in the fridge to pickle for at least 2 hours or overnight to pickle, stirring or squidging occasionally.

Quarter the melon, discard the seeds and remove the flesh from the skin. Use the melon baller to scoop out 32 balls from the flesh and set these aside. Alternatively, simply slice the flesh into 32 x 1cm dice. Roughly chop the remaining flesh and pop it into a food processor or blender. Add the ginger and lemon juice. Blitz for 1 minute until as smooth as possible. Season to taste with a little salt. Pour into a large jug, cover and chill in the fridge for at least 1 hour or overnight, until well chilled. This can be made up to two days in advance.

Divide the soup evenly between wide, shallow bowls. Drain the prawns and cucumber and discard the lime leaf. Arrange three prawns in the centre of each bowl, then top with pickled cucumber and the reserved melon balls or pieces. Drizzle with a little olive oil, garnish with mint sprigs and serve.

FOR A TWIST...

- Instead of the pickled toppings, garnish with crumbled feta or goats' cheese.

- Serve in a fun and frosty 'ice bowl', as shown in the photo. These are made by placing a small bowl inside a larger bowl and freezing water in the gap between them. For a pretty effect, pack the water full of lime slices, herbs or edible flowers, before freezing. To remove, very briefly run first the outer and then the inner bowl under hot water.

BEETROOT, COCONUT & LEMONGRASS SOUP

Ⓥ ⒼⒻ

This makes a deliciously smooth and velvety soup, with a vibrant colour to boot. The Asian spices take the earthy beetroot flavour to another level. It's important to use a jug blender rather than a food processor for this recipe, to make sure you get a very smooth finish.

SERVES 6

500g cooked beetroot and juices (from a vacuum pack, not in vinegar)
Vegetable or chicken stock cube, powder or concentrate (enough for 275ml stock)
175ml coconut milk
1 stick of lemongrass
Thumb-sized piece of fresh ginger, peeled
1 garlic clove, peeled
1 red chilli, de-seeded if you prefer
Grated or pared zest and juice of 1 lime
Sea salt and freshly ground black pepper

TO SERVE:

15g toasted, dried coconut shavings
Small handful of fresh coriander and/or baby red chard leaves
Flatbreads, naan breads or lentil crisps (choose gluten-free options if necessary)

ESSENTIAL KIT:
Kettle
Jug blender

Put the kettle on to boil, about a quarter full.

Cut 25g of the beetroot into tiny dice and reserve for serving. Roughly chop the remaining beetroot and pop it in a blender with any juices. Make the stock up with 275ml of just-boiled water and pour that into the blender, along with 150ml of the coconut milk. Roughly chop the lemongrass, ginger, garlic and chilli, then add to the blender along with the lime juice. Blitz for 1–2 minutes until really smooth.

Season to taste. Pour into a large jug, cover and place in the fridge for at least 1 hour or overnight, until well chilled. This can be made up to two days in advance.

Ladle the soup into wide, shallow serving bowls and drizzle with the remaining 25ml of coconut milk. Scatter the reserved diced beetroot across the centre, followed by the coconut shavings and then the lime zest. Garnish with coriander and/or red chard leaves and serve with flatbreads, naan breads or lentil crisps.

GAZPACHO

(V) (GF)

Gazpacho, the classic chilled tomato soup, is so quick and easy to make, with an amazingly fresh and summery taste. In no time, you'll have a delicious, healthy, low-fat lunch. Sherry vinegar is traditional, but you can use red wine vinegar or even lemon juice if you prefer. For a smoother, silkier texture, pass the gazpacho through a fine sieve. If you can't find ripe tomatoes, you can use any type of tinned ones. You can also substitute the fresh chilli with dried flakes or hot pepper sauce (such as Tabasco), and beef up the soup a little with a dash of Worcester sauce if you like.

SERVES 4

400g vine-ripened tomatoes (about 4 medium), roughly chopped
125g cucumber, roughly chopped
1 small red pepper, de-seeded
1 small yellow pepper, de-seeded
½ small red onion, peeled
1 small garlic clove, peeled and roughly chopped
½ red chilli, roughly chopped, de-seeded if you prefer less heat (optional)
Small handful of fresh basil leaves
½ tsp sherry vinegar
½ small avocado
1 tbsp extra virgin olive oil
8 tiny, fresh mint leaves
Sea salt and freshly ground black pepper

ESSENTIAL KIT:
Jug blender

Place the tomatoes and cucumber into the blender. Roughly chop three-quarters of each pepper and half the red onion (i.e. one-quarter of an onion) and add to the blender, along with the garlic, chilli (if using), basil and sherry vinegar. Blitz everything until smooth and then season to taste. Pour into a jug, cover and chill in the fridge for at least 1 hour. This can be made up to one day in advance and will just need a stir before serving.

When ready to serve, prepare the toppings. Very finely chop the remaining peppers and red onion. Peel the avocado (discarding the stone if necessary) and chop the flesh very finely.

Pour the gazpacho into small serving bowls, cups or glasses and scatter with the prepared toppings. Drizzle a little olive oil on top. Garnish with two mint leaves each and serve.

FOR A TWIST...
- Try other tasty toppings, such as cooked crab meat or finely chopped cooked prawns, finely chopped chives, grated boiled egg, crumbled croutons or an ice cube for extra chill.

- Serve the gazpacho with an oyster on the side.

CREAMY CORN & CHICKEN SOUP
with corn rows

GF

This is a velouté-style soup, meaning it is silky smooth, so it is important to use a jug blender rather than a food processor to ensure as fine a blend as possible. For a more rustic-style soup, simply omit passing it through a sieve. It will also result in slightly bigger portions that way.

SERVES 4

600g sweetcorn kernels (drained or defrosted weight)
100g cashew nuts
2 celery sticks, roughly chopped
Chicken or vegetable stock cube, powder or concentrate (enough for 300ml stock)
75g cooked chicken (smoked if you like), finely diced
Small handful of fresh chives
1 corn cake or 25g salted popcorn
Sea salt and freshly ground black pepper

ESSENTIAL KIT:
Kettle
Jug blender

Half-fill the kettle with water and put it on to boil.

Place 500g of the sweetcorn in a blender with the cashew nuts and celery. Make up the stock with 300ml of just-boiled water. Pour into the blender and blitz for 1–2 minutes until as smooth as possible. Be extremely careful when blending hot liquid.

Pass the soup through a fine sieve over a large jug or bowl, pressing with the back of a spoon until the remaining pulp is as dry as possible. Discard the pulp and season the soup to taste. It can be served straight away, or cover and place in the fridge for at least 1 hour or overnight, until chilled. This can be made up to two days in advance.

When ready to serve, pour or ladle the soup evenly between four wide, shallow soup plates. Scatter a quarter of the remaining 100g of sweetcorn in a thin row across one side of each soup. Scatter a row of chicken beside the corn, followed by a row of chives. Finish with a row of crumbled corn cake or salted popcorn. Serve at once, unless you wish to serve it chilled.

FOR A TWIST...
- Top the soup with crumbled-up croutons instead of corn cakes or popcorn, if not intolerant to gluten.

SALADS

GREEN CAULIFLOWER-RICE BUDDHA BOWL
with spiced chickpeas & zingy carrot dressing

(V) (GF)

A buddha bowl is a healthy but hearty salad of greens, beans and grains. Here, the 'grain' is cauliflower blitzed to resemble rice, a tasty, no-cook shortcut that is also carb-free. If you can't get fresh beetroot, replace with 500g of cooked beetroot from a vacuum pack (not in vinegar). Dried seaweed sprinkles, e.g. dillisk or dulse, can be found in many Asian or health food stores.

SERVES 4

1 small cauliflower
50g kale
Handful of flat-leaf parsley
25g goji berries or dried cranberries
25g pumpkin or sunflower seeds
1 x 400g can chickpeas
2 tbsp extra virgin olive oil
½ tsp ground cumin
½ tsp cayenne pepper
2 fresh beetroots
2 ripe avocados
25g sprouted peas or salad cress
½ tsp seaweed sprinkles (optional)
Sea salt and freshly ground black pepper

DRESSING:

5cm of fresh ginger, peeled
50ml extra virgin olive oil
50ml carrot juice
25ml apple cider vinegar
2 tsp almond butter
1 tsp honey
⅛ tsp turmeric powder

ESSENTIAL KIT:

Food processor
Spiraliser (or grater)

Break the cauliflower into florets and place in a food processor. Remove any hard spines from the kale and add two-thirds of the leaves, reserving the rest for serving. Pick the parsley leaves, add to the processor and blitz for about 30 seconds until the cauliflower resembles rice and the mixture is speckled green. Tip into a large bowl, add the dried berries and seeds, and toss everything together well. Season to taste and set aside.

Drain and rinse the chickpeas and place them in a medium bowl. Add the oil and spices and toss together until evenly coated. Season to taste.

To make the dressing, finely grate the ginger and place in a screw-cap jar with the oil, carrot juice, vinegar, almond butter, honey and turmeric. Secure the lid and shake until well blended. Season and set aside.

Peel the beetroots and pass them through a spiraliser to give nice curls, or just roughly grate them. Quarter the avocados, discard the skin and stone and cut each piece into slices.

To assemble, divide the cauliflower rice and spiced chickpeas between serving bowls. Arrange the beetroot and the avocado slices to one side. Add a pile of the sprouted peas and the reserved kale, torn into small pieces. Drizzle some of the dressing over the top and serve the rest on the side in a small jug. Dust with dried seaweed sprinkles if you like, and serve.

FOR A TWIST...

- Instead of dried seaweed sprinkles, you can simply crumble a nori seaweed sheet, which are sold in many supermakets.

- The Beetroot & Bean Sliders (page 137), Falafel (page 128) or Quinoa & Spinach No-meat Balls (page 114) all make a wonderful addition to this bowl.

BRUSSELS SPROUT SALAD

with bacon, pecans, cranberries & maple dressing

(GF)

Brussels sprouts have a hard time in the popularity stakes, thanks to how often they are overcooked or boiled to death. However, because the sprouts in this recipe aren't cooked at all, just finely shredded, they are almost unrecognisable – not just in appearance but in flavour too, which is beautifully fresh and sweet. The addition of maple syrup and vanilla seeds accentuates this, and contrasts deliciously with the salty, crisp bacon. Give this salad a whirl and you'll have a sprout recipe for life, not just for Christmas.

SERVES 2 (OR 4 AS A SIDE)
250g Brussels sprouts
50g dried cranberries
50g pecan nuts, roughly chopped
Small handful of fresh chives, finely chopped
4 strips of cooked crispy streaky bacon (smoked or unsmoked)
Sea salt and freshly ground black pepper

MAPLE DRESSING:
4 tbsp olive oil
2 tbsp white wine vinegar
1 tsp maple syrup
Seeds from ½ vanilla pod or ½ tsp vanilla bean paste

ESSENTIAL KIT:
Mandolin or food processor set with slicing blade (or sharp knife)

To make the dressing, pour the oil, vinegar and maple syrup into a large bowl with the vanilla seeds or bean paste. Whisk together until blended and set aside.

Trim the Brussels sprouts and finely shred them on a mandolin (carefully!), in a food processor, or by hand with a sharp knife. Put into a bowl and pour over the dressing, then add the cranberries, pecans and chopped chives. Crumble in the bacon and give everything a good toss together. Season to taste.

Divide between serving plates or bowls and enjoy straight away. If making in advance, only toss in the dressing just before serving to avoid the salad becoming soggy.

FOR A TWIST...
- Omit the bacon strips and add cooked chestnuts for a vegetarian version.

WALDORF SALAD
with smoked ham & buttermilk dressing

GF

This all-American salad originated in New York's Waldorf Astoria Hotel in the 1800s. It traditionally has a mayonnaise dressing, but this variation uses buttermilk and yoghurt for a lighter, tangier edge. Pickled eggs and smoked ham are the no-cook cheat ingredients here, helping to make this a super-speedy dish. Buy the best-quality smoked ham you can. Slicing the apple without removing the core gives a pretty star shape in the centre of the slices, but you can remove the core if you prefer.

SERVES 4

100g red or green or
 mixed grapes
100g watercress
1 celery stick
1 Granny Smith apple or
 Braeburn apple
16 thin smoked ham slices
2 pickled eggs
25g walnuts or walnut
 pieces
Sea salt and freshly ground
 black pepper

BUTTERMILK DRESSING:

100ml buttermilk
50g Greek yoghurt
½ tsp poppy seeds
¼ tsp Dijon mustard
Juice of ½ lemon

To make the dressing, pour the buttermilk into a large bowl and add the yoghurt, poppy seeds, mustard and lemon juice. Whisk everything together until well blended. Season to taste and set aside. This can be made up to two days in advance and kept covered in the fridge.

Halve the grapes and discard any tough stalks from the watercress. Toss them both into the bowl of dressing. Using a vegetable peeler, shave the celery stick into long thin ribbons and add these. Very thinly slice the apple horizontally across the core, flicking the seeds out as you go. Add the slices to the bowl and toss everything together gently, until evenly coated.

Divide the ham between the serving plates, arranging four slices in a single layer all over each one. Pile the dressed salad into the centre of each plate, on top of the ham. Quarter the eggs and arrange two pieces on each plate. Break up the walnuts, sprinkle over the top and serve.

FOR A TWIST...

- While not strictly a Waldorf, omit the ham to make vegtarian-friendly. It can be replaced with sliced vegetarian cheddar, if you like.

PARMA HAM & KALE CAESAR SALAD

The croute base of this salad is made from toast, which acts as a crunchy platform for the crisp lettuce, luscious dressing and salty Parma and Parmesan fusion. You can also use shop-bought bruschetta if your supermarket or deli sells it. The Caesar dressing contains raw egg, so it is unsuitable for very young children or for anyone pregnant or frail.

SERVES 4

8 slices of crusty bread (such as wholegrain or sourdough)
100g kale
1 head cos lettuce
25g Parmesan cheese
8 slices of Parma ham
25g toasted pine nuts
Sea salt and freshly ground black pepper

CAESAR DRESSING:

1 large egg
2 tsp English mustard powder
2 anchovies
Few shakes of Worcester sauce
1 small garlic clove, peeled and roughly chopped
Juice of ½ lemon
150ml olive oil

ESSENTIAL KIT:

Jug blender
Toaster

To make the dressing, crack the egg into a blender and add the mustard powder, anchovies, Worcester sauce, garlic and lemon juice. Turn the blender on and gradually pour the oil through the feeder hole until all has been added and you have a smooth, thick dressing. Season to taste. This can be made up to three days in advance and kept covered in the fridge. When ready to use, pour three-quarters of the dressing into a large bowl and reserve the remainder.

Working in batches if necessary, toast the bread slices in a toaster until golden. Arrange two on each serving plate.

Remove any thick stalks from the kale and discard. Tear the leaves and add to the large bowl of dressing. Trim the cos lettuce, cut across the head into 2cm thick slices and add. Finely grate two-thirds of the Parmesan and sprinkle in. Toss everything together well, until evenly coated.

Pile the salad on top of each toast croute and top each one with a ruffle of Parma ham. Drizzle with the remaining dressing and scatter with the pine nuts. Shave the remaining Parmesan on top and serve at once.

FOR A TWIST...
• Use cooked prawns or chicken instead of Parma ham.

CELERIAC & HAZELNUT SLAW
with smoked mackerel

GF

Celeriac may be a somewhat ugly vegetable, but its nutty, celery-like flavour is truly delicious, so give it a chance. Besides being great cooked, its firm texture and strong flavour make it an excellent choice to use raw for a slaw. Smoked mackerel is often sold with different flavourings such as black pepper or chilli – a wholegrain mustard or pepper-flavoured one works well with this recipe.

SERVES 4

150g mayonnaise
1 tbsp Dijon mustard
Finely grated zest and juice of 1 lemon
50g capers, roughly chopped
Large handful of fresh flat-leaf parsley leaves
Large handful of fresh tarragon leaves
50g roasted hazelnuts, roughly chopped
1 celeriac (about 1kg)
1 large red-skinned apple
4 smoked mackerel fillets
Sea salt and freshly ground black pepper

ESSENTIAL KIT:
Mandolin, julienne peeler or long, sharp knife

Spoon the mayonnaise and mustard into a large bowl, and add the lemon zest and juice and capers. Reserve a small handful of the parsley and tarragon leaves, roughly chop the rest and add, along with half the hazelnuts. Give everything a good stir together until well blended. Season to taste and set aside.

Peel the celeriac, cut into manageable chunks and then slice into small matchsticks using a mandolin, julienne peeler or a long, sharp knife. Toss into the dressing as you go, to prevent it from discolouring.

Quarter the apple, remove the core and cut the flesh into small matchsticks. Toss this through the slaw mixture too. Adjust the seasoning, if necessary. This can be made up to a few hours in advance.

Divide the slaw between four serving plates or bowls. Remove the skin and any dark residue from the mackerel fillets and flake the flesh over each one. Scatter the reserved parsley, tarragon and hazelnuts on top and serve at once.

FOR A TWIST...

- Replace the mackerel with hot smoked trout or salmon, or cooked ham. Or omit for a vegetarian version.

- Use gherkins instead of capers.

- Use pear instead of apple.

BEEF, BLUEBERRY & FETA SALAD

(GF)

Combining beef and blueberries in a salad might sound unusual, but they make a surprisingly happy couple. The vinegar in the dressing cuts through the sweetness of the fruit, while the distinctive taste of feta pulls everything together. Try to source good-quality beef slices that are nice and pink – the meat in the photo is spiced beef. Speaking of happy couples, this is a great starter for a romantic meal or dinner party – just increase the quantities if you've got guests. If not eating straight away, keep the dressing separate until ready to serve.

SERVES 2

125g blueberries
2 tbsp extra virgin olive oil
1 tbsp redcurrant jelly
1 tsp red wine vinegar
1 x 215g can chickpeas
75g mixed salad leaves
Small handful of fresh mint leaves
25g roasted hazelnuts, roughly chopped
125g cooked beef slices
100g feta cheese
Sea salt and freshly ground black pepper

ESSENTIAL KIT:
Mini-blender

Place half the blueberries in a mini-blender with the oil, redcurrant jelly and vinegar. Blitz until as smooth as possible. Season to taste.

Drain and rinse the chickpeas and place them in a large bowl with the remaining blueberries, the salad leaves, mint and hazelnuts. Chop or tear the beef into bite-sized pieces if necessary and add to the bowl. Give everything a good toss.

Divide between serving plates or bowls and crumble the feta cheese on top. Drizzle with the dressing and serve immediately.

FIVE-SPICED DUCK NOODLE SALAD
with pak choi slaw

The flavours of duck and five spice (an aromatic Chinese flavouring) are a marriage made in heaven. Roasted crispy half-ducks are available in the chilled section of most supermarkets. Serving your salad in a red cabbage 'bowl' adds some extra fun for special occasions.

SERVES 4
250g thin rice noodles
Juice of 2 limes
2 tbsp olive oil
2 tbsp fish sauce
1 tbsp soy sauce
¼ tsp five spice
5cm piece of ginger, peeled
1 garlic clove, peeled
150g cooked duck meat, finely shredded (from a roasted crispy half-duck)
3 spring onions, finely sliced
1 red chilli, finely sliced
Large handful of fresh coriander leaves
8 large red cabbage leaves
1 lime, quartered

PAK CHOI SLAW:
100g natural yoghurt
1 tsp soy sauce
Juice of 1 lime
2 large heads of pak choi
Large handful of fresh mint leaves, roughly chopped
50g salted peanuts, roughly chopped
100g beansprouts

ESSENTIAL KIT:
Kettle

Fill a kettle with water and put it on to boil.

For the slaw, place the yoghurt, soy sauce and lime juice in a large bowl, and mix together. Trim and finely shred the pak choi. Prepare all the other ingredients and set aside, ready to assemble and toss just before serving.

Lay the noodles in a wide dish and pour over enough just-boiled water to cover. Cover and leave to soak for 8–10 minutes (or according to the packet instructions) until tender, stirring halfway through.

To make the dressing for the noodles, pour the lime juice, oil, fish and soy sauces into a large bowl and add the five spice. Finely grate the ginger and crush the garlic, then add both to the bowl and mix everything together well. Add the duck, spring onions and chilli. Reserve a small handful of coriander leaves and add the rest to the dressing. Toss everything, until evenly coated.

Once tender, drain the noodles and refresh under cold running water. Add them to the duck salad and toss them through.

Reserving half the peanuts for a garnish, add the rest of the slaw ingredients to the yoghurt dressing. Toss together well.

Arrange two red cabbage leaves on each serving plate as edible bowls. Pile the slaw into one and the duck noodles into the other. Scatter with the remaining peanuts and coriander, and serve with the lime wedges.

FOR A TWIST...
- To make this gluten-free, replace the soy sauce with tamari and choose a gluten-free fish sauce.

CHICKEN CHOW MEIN NOODLE SALAD

Pre-cooked noodles are usually found in the fridge section of supermarkets and are sold ready to eat. This salad makes a perfect picnic or lunchbox treat that your kids are sure to love. If you can't find toasted sesame seeds, just use regular ones.

SERVES 4

1 x 400g bag pre-cooked egg noodles

125g beansprouts

250g cooked chicken

3 spring onions, finely sliced

125g mangetout, finely sliced

1 red pepper, de-seeded and finely sliced

Large handful of fresh coriander leaves, roughly chopped

1 tbsp toasted sesame seeds

SAUCE:

3 tbsp oyster sauce

3 tbsp light soy sauce

3 tbsp sweet chilli sauce

½ tsp sesame oil

Juice of 1 lime

1 garlic clove, peeled and crushed

Thumb-sized piece of fresh ginger, peeled and finely grated

To make the sauce, pour the oyster, soy and chilli sauces and sesame oil into a large bowl. Add the lime juice, garlic and ginger. Mix everything together until well blended.

Pop the noodles and beansprouts in on top of the sauce. Tear the chicken into bite-sized pieces and add, along with the spring onions, mangetout, pepper and coriander leaves. Toss everything together until well mixed.

Pile onto serving plates, or into lunchboxes, and sprinkle with sesame seeds. This can be made up to one day in advance and kept covered in the fridge.

FOR A TWIST...

- Use pre-cooked prawns as an alternative to chicken.

- Omit the chicken to make a vegetarian version, adding green beans or peas instead, if you prefer.

LENTIL, PEACH & HALLOUMI PANZANELLA
with walnut dressing

Ⓥ

Panzanella is a Tuscan salad made from stale bread and tomatoes. Here, fresh sweet peaches are used in place of the usual tomatoes. The bread really does need to be stale or it goes soggy very quickly. If your loaf is not already stale, tear it into small pieces and scatter on a large tray. Leave aside, uncovered, for about 1 hour to dry out. Only dress the salad when ready to serve or the bread will absorb all the liquid.

SERVES 4

2 x 400g cans or 2 x 250g
    pouches of cooked
    lentils
125g roasted red peppers
    (from a jar), roughly
    chopped
2 peaches
100g halloumi cheese
100g stale ciabatta bread
75g wild rocket or mixed
    salad leaves
Small handful of fresh
    basil leaves
Sea salt and freshly ground
    black pepper

DRESSING:

75ml olive oil
75ml walnut oil
50ml cider vinegar
50g walnuts, finely chopped
Small handful of fresh
    chives, finely chopped
2 tsp Dijon mustard

To make the dressing, pour the oils and vinegar into a screw-cap jar. Add the walnuts, chives and mustard. Secure the lid on top and shake vigorously to combine. Season to taste.

Pour half the dressing into a large bowl. Drain and rinse the lentils if necessary, and add to the bowl along with the peppers. Quarter the peaches, discard the stones and cut the flesh into slices. Cut the halloumi into small cubes and tear the bread into bite-sized pieces. Add all these to the bowl, along with the rocket or salad leaves. Toss everything gently until evenly coated.

Pile the salad onto serving plates or bowls. Scatter with the basil leaves, and serve with the remaining dressing on the side in a small jug.

FOR A TWIST...
- Use feta or goats' cheese instead of halloumi.

VEGETARIAN DISHES

QUINOA & SPINACH NO-MEAT BALLS
with carrot 'spaghetti' & tahini sauce

(V) (GF)

This super-healthy vegetarian take on spaghetti with meatballs couldn't be easier to make, using a pouch of pre-cooked quinoa (white, red or mixed), available in supermarkets and health food stores. Kids will love to help spiralise the carrot and roll the balls. For instant gratification, you can also serve the balls as a snack with your favourite dip.

SERVES 4

1 x 250g pouch of cooked
    quinoa (in any colour)
50g ground almonds
1 tbsp tahini paste
Big pinch of grated nutmeg
1 garlic clove, peeled and
    roughly chopped
Small handful of fresh chives
125g frozen spinach, thawed
½ tsp black or toasted
    white sesame seeds
10g sprouted peas or salad
    cress
Sea salt and freshly ground
    black pepper

CARROT 'SPAGHETTI':

75g tahini paste
1 tbsp extra virgin olive oil
1 tsp clear honey
Big pinch of cayenne pepper
Juice of 1 lemon
Finely grated zest and
    juice of 1 orange
2 large carrots, peeled

ESSENTIAL KIT:

Spiraliser, mandolin or
    julienne/vegetable
    peeler
Food processor

Line a small tray with non-stick baking paper and set aside.

First, prepare the dressing for the 'spaghetti'. Place the tahini, olive oil, honey and cayenne pepper in a large bowl with the lemon juice and orange zest and juice. Whisk everything together well and season to taste.

Shred the carrots into long thin matchsticks using a spiraliser, mandolin or julienne peeler. Alternatively, slice into strips with a vegetable peeler. Toss the carrot through the tahini dressing and set aside.

Place half the quinoa in a food processor with the almonds, tahini, nutmeg and garlic. Roughly chop the chives and add them too. Squeeze the spinach dry, add it to the processor and blitz to give a fairly fine mixture. Transfer to a large bowl and stir the remaining quinoa through until well combined – this is easiest to do with clean hands. Season to taste.

Using damp hands, shape the mixture into 20 balls (weighing about 20g each). Lay them on the prepared tray as you go. These can be made up to two days in advance and kept covered in the fridge, or they can also be frozen.

Pile the carrot spaghetti in the centre of each serving plate and drizzle any remaining dressing over. Arrange the no-meat balls on top. Scatter with the sesame seeds and sprouted peas or cress, and serve.

BLACK BEAN BURGER

with pickled red onion, chipotle cream & sweetcorn salad

Ⓥ

For a truly tasty vegetarian burger, look no further. This bean burger has a robust and meaty texture that even carnivores will love. Chipotle sauce gives a rich smoky flavour to the sour cream, and is an authentic Mexican accompaniment to black beans, but any hot chilli sauce will work if you can't find it.

SERVES 4
100g cooked brown rice (from a pouch)
25g pumpkin seeds
2 x 400g cans black beans
1 small garlic clove, peeled
Finely grated zest of 1 lime
½ tsp smoked paprika
½ tbsp ground cumin
Small handful of fresh coriander leaves
4 burger buns
75g sour cream
Few shakes of chipotle or other hot chilli sauce
1 ripe avocado
Sea salt and freshly ground black pepper

PICKLED RED ONION:
2 tbsp white wine vinegar
2 tsp caster sugar
1 red onion, peeled and finely sliced into rings

see opposite for more ➜

Put the kettle on to boil, about a quarter full.

To pickle the onion, stir the vinegar and sugar together in a small bowl or shake in a resealable food bag until the sugar dissolves. Add the red onion to the bowl or bag and toss until well coated. Leave to soak while you prepare everything else, stirring or shaking occasionally.

To make the burgers, place the rice in a small bowl and pour over enough just-boiled water to cover. Cover and leave to soak for 5 minutes.

Blitz the pumpkin seeds for the burger in a food processor until fairly finely chopped. Spread out on a large plate, set aside, and wipe out the processor.

Drain the black beans, rinse well and place in the food processor. Roughly chop the garlic clove and add to the processor along with the lime zest, paprika, cumin and coriander. Drain the rice well and add. Blitz to a rough paste, but keeping some texture. Season to taste. Divide the mixture into four even-sized portions (about 150g each) and shape each one into a 4cm-thick burger patty. Transfer to a plate, cover and chill in the fridge for at least 30 minutes to firm up a little. These can be made up to two days in advance.

In a medium bowl, mix together the sweetcorn, mayonnaise, Parmesan, lime zest and juice. Finely chop the coriander leaves and stir through all but a small handful. Season to taste. Spoon into a serving bowl, sprinkle over the remaining coriander and set aside until needed.

continued opposite

SWEETCORN SALAD:

575g sweetcorn kernels (drained or defrosted weight)

100g mayonnaise

25g vegetarian hard cheese, finely grated

Finely grated zest and juice of 1 lime

Small handful of fresh coriander leaves

ESSENTIAL KIT:

Kettle

Food processor

Toaster

When ready to serve, toast the buns in a toaster until golden brown. Dip each burger patty into the blitzed pumpkin seeds and coat evenly. Place the sour cream in a small bowl and add enough chilli sauce to taste. Finally, quarter the avocado, discard the skin and stone, and cut each piece into slices.

Spread a little of the chipotle sour cream on each bun base and arrange the avocado slices on top. Sit a burger on each one and spoon more sour cream over the top. Drain the red onions from the pickling liquid and pile them onto each burger. Top with the other half of the bun and serve with the sweetcorn salad.

FOR A TWIST...

- Make cheesy corn cobs instead of the sweetcorn salad, if you can find vacuum-packed cooked corn cobs. Cut four cobs into three pieces each and roll them through the same mayonnaise dressing (without the cheese). Scatter 50g grated hard cheese in a wide bowl, then roll the cobs through it to stick.

- For a gluten-free option, replace the burger buns with marinated mushrooms (page 123).

HERBY SOFT CHEESE TART

with nutty pastry, grapes & watercress

Ⓥ ⒼⒻ

This tart is filled with a delicious homemade soft cheese known as labneh, a super-easy Middle Eastern recipe made by straining yoghurt. It's very simple but you do need to start a couple of days in advance. The whey that gets strained off the yoghurt is filled with nutrients and is great for the digestive system, so use it in a smoothie, as a salad dressing or in place of milk in the 'Carrot Cake' Overnight Oats (page 35). For a speedier (although not quite as tasty) filling, use 500g shop-bought cream cheese instead. The pastry in this recipe is made from blended nuts and seeds; it's a quick, gluten-free alternative that requires no cooking.

SERVES 4–6

750g full-fat Greek yoghurt
**½ tsp fine sea salt or
  celery salt**
**Really large handful of
  fresh flat-leaf parsley
  leaves or chives (or a
  mix), finely chopped**
**1 small garlic clove, peeled
  and crushed**
**175g each of red and green
  seedless grapes, halved**
75g watercress
Pinch of celery salt (optional)

PINE NUT PASTRY:

100g toasted pine nuts
100g sunflower seeds
50g walnuts
25g linseed
**50g sun-dried tomatoes
  (from a jar)**
**1 tbsp extra virgin olive oil
  (or oil from sun-dried
  tomato jar)**
Juice of ½ lemon
**Sea salt and freshly ground
  black pepper**

turn for more →

Line a large sieve (or colander) with a double layer of cheesecloth, leaving extra to hang over the edge. Set it over a large bowl, deep enough to leave a few inches between the bottom of the sieve and the base of the bowl.

Place the yoghurt in a large bowl and stir the salt through it, then pour it into the sieve. Spread it level and flip the excess cheesecloth over the top to cover. Chill in the fridge for at least 8 hours or overnight. The yoghurt is ready when the whey has dripped out into the bowl, leaving a thick and creamy 'cheese' in the cloth. The longer the yoghurt is left, the thicker the finished cheese will be.

To make the tart case, blitz the pine nuts, sunflower seeds, walnuts and linseed in a food processor until fairly fine. Add the sun-dried tomatoes, oil and lemon juice. Blitz again to give a rough, moist and sticky mixture. Season to taste. Tip the mixture into the tin and press it in evenly. Cover and chill in the fridge for at least 3 hours or overnight, until set firm. This can be made up to two days in advance.

When all the whey has dripped out of the yoghurt, flip the resulting thick 'cheese' out of the cloth into a medium bowl. Stir in the chopped parsley or chives (or both) and garlic and season to taste. Spread the mixture evenly into the tart case. Carefully remove the tart from the tin onto a long serving platter. Arrange the red and green grape halves in alternate diagonal rows along the length of the tart. This can be assembled a day ahead.

continued overleaf

4 tbsp extra virgin olive oil

1 tbsp sherry or red wine vinegar

1 tsp Dijon mustard

¼ tsp clear honey

1 shallot, peeled and finely chopped

2 x 40cm square pieces of cheesecloth or muslin

Food processor

10cm x 32cm fluted, loose-bottomed tart tin (2.5cm in height)

When you're ready to serve, make the dressing by whisking the oil, vinegar, mustard and honey together in a large bowl until thickened. Stir in the shallot and season to taste.

Remove any very woody stems from the watercress and toss the rest through the dressing just before serving. Scatter the dressed watercress on top of the tart, drizzle with any remaining dressing and sprinkle over a pinch of celery salt, if you like.

FOR A TWIST...

- Shape the soft cheese into small balls and marinate in a jar of flavoured oil, or use instead of the blue cheese in the Blue Cheese and Bacon Truffle Pops (page 59).

LENTIL & KALE POT PIES
with fresh tomato salad

(V) (GF)

These alternative pot pies are topped with a no-cook, gluten-free 'pastry' lid made from nuts, seeds and sun-dried tomatoes. It does need a little time to firm up in the fridge, but the rest of the dish is very quick to assemble if everything is prepared in advance. For a fun finishing touch, you can cut the lids into shapes with cookie cutters before popping on top of the pies.

SERVES 4

75g kale

75g toasted pine nuts

75ml extra virgin olive oil

Large handful of fresh basil leaves

1 garlic clove, peeled and roughly chopped

Juice of ½ lemon

25g vegetarian hard cheese, finely grated

2 x 400g cans or 2 x 250g pouches of cooked lentils (any type)

'PASTRY' TOPPING:

100g roasted hazelnuts (whole or chopped)

50g almonds

75g sunflower seeds

25g milled flaxseed (also known as ground linseed)

75g sun-dried tomatoes (from a jar)

1 tbsp extra virgin olive oil (or oil from sun-dried tomato jar)

Juice of ½ lemon

Sea salt and freshly ground black pepper

turn for more →

Line a tray with non-stick baking paper and set aside.

To make the 'pastry' topping, place the hazelnuts, almonds and sunflower seeds in a food processor and blitz them until the consistency is fairly fine. Add the flaxseed, sun-dried tomatoes, oil and lemon juice. Blitz again to give a rough, moist and sticky mixture. Season to taste.

Turn out the mixture onto a large sheet of baking paper and place another sheet on top. Roll out the pastry, between the papers, into a 26cm circle, about 3mm thick. Remove the top sheet and, using an inverted serving dish as a template, cut out four circles as pie tops. They may be a little crumbly so use a wide fish slice to lift them and transfer carefully to the lined tray. Cover and chill in the fridge for at least 3 hours or overnight, until set firm. These can be made up to two days in advance.

To make a kale pesto, remove any tough stalks from the kale and pop the leaves in a food processor. Add the pine nuts, oil, basil, garlic and lemon juice. Blitz to a paste and then spoon out into a large bowl. Add the Parmesan and give the pesto a good stir. Season to taste. This is best prepared on the day you intend to serve the pies.

Drain and rinse the lentils if using canned ones (those in pouches are ready to use). Pour them into the kale pesto and toss until well coated. Spoon the mixture into the serving dishes and top each one with a firmed-up circle of the pie topping, pressing down the edges to secure. These are best eaten on the day they are assembled and served at room temperature, rather

continued overleaf

TOMATO SALAD:

600g ripe mixed tomatoes
Large handful of fresh
basil leaves, torn
6 tbsp extra virgin olive oil
2 tbsp balsamic vinegar

ESSENTIAL KIT:

4 x 250ml individual
serving dishes, about
12cm wide and 4cm
deep
Food processor
Rolling pin

than fridge-cold.

Finally, to prepare the tomato salad, roughly chop, slice or wedge the tomatoes and place in a large bowl with the torn basil. Drizzle with the oil and vinegar, and season with salt and pepper. Using clean hands, toss everything together until well mixed and coated.

Place each pie dish on a serving plate, arrange some tomato salad alongside and serve.

FOR A TWIST...

- For a non-veggie version, add chopped pieces of crispy, cooked, smoked bacon to the kale and lentil mix.

- Toss the kale pesto through pasta.

- Use the pie tops as tart bases. Arrange tomato and mozzarella slices on top and finish with either the kale pesto or the standard basil variety.

CHESTNUT, BLUE CHEESE & WATERCRESS PIZZAS
on marinated mushroom bases

(V) (GF)

This bread-free twist on pizza consists of toppings loaded onto delicious marinated Portobello mushrooms. Marinating mushrooms is a convenient way of 'cooking' them without actually turning on the heat. The marinade can even be re-used for a second batch of mushrooms. The beetroot pâté on page 70 makes a great alternative to the watercress pesto, if you prefer.

SERVES 4

200ml extra virgin olive oil
4 tbsp balsamic vinegar
Juice of 2 lemons
1 large red onion, peeled and finely chopped
4 garlic cloves, peeled and finely chopped
Large handful of fresh tarragon leaves, roughly chopped
8 large portobello (or other flat) mushrooms
4 tsp balsamic glaze
4 small pickled onions, quartered
175g blue cheese
8 cooked, peeled chestnuts
50g watercress

WATERCRESS PESTO:
100g watercress
1 small garlic clove, peeled and roughly chopped
25g toasted flaked almonds
5 tbsp extra virgin olive oil
Finely grated zest of 1 lemon
Sea salt and freshly ground black pepper

ESSENTIAL KIT:
Food processor

First, marinate the mushrooms. Place the oil, vinegar and lemon juice in a large, wide dish or resealable food bag (if using a bag, sit it in a large jug or bowl to prevent spillages when filling up). Add the onion, garlic and chopped tarragon. Pour in 250ml of cold water and whisk or shake everything together.

Discard the stalks from the mushrooms and drop the tops into the bag or dish, tossing them through the marinade to coat. Cover or seal and chill in the fridge for at least 4 hours or overnight, until softened. These can be made up to two days in advance.

To make the pesto, discard any tough stems from the watercress and pop the rest in a food processor. Add the garlic, almonds, olive oil and lemon zest, and blitz to give a fairly smooth paste. Season to taste and set aside. This can be made up to two days ahead and kept in the fridge.

When the mushrooms are marinated, drain well and arrange two on each serving plate. Divide the watercress pesto evenly between the mushrooms and spread it out to cover the surface. Sit two quarters of a pickled onion on each mushroom, crumble the blue cheese and chestnuts over the top, and drizzle around each pair with a teaspoon of balsamic glaze. Discard any tough stems from the watercress and scatter it on top to serve.

FOR A TWIST...

- For a non-vegetarian version, crumble crispy cooked smoked bacon over the top.

- Once marinated, the mushrooms also make great gluten-free 'burger buns'.

WATERMELON PIZZA
with fig, feta & raspberry dressing

(V) (GF)

A watermelon pizza might sound a bit bonkers, but this colourful mix of sweet and savoury is a flavour sensation and will be the talk of the table whenever and wherever you serve it. It's a perfect vegetarian and gluten-free treat for a summer garden party or girls' night in, and will definitely be the healthiest pizza you have ever eaten!

SERVES 2 (OR 4 AS A STARTER)

2 x round watermelon slices, about 20cm in diameter, 2cm thick
2 ripe yellow, orange or red tomatoes, thinly sliced
2 fresh figs
100g feta cheese
50g pitted black olives, halved
25g roasted hazelnuts, roughly chopped
Small handful of fresh mint leaves
Small handful of fresh wild rocket
Sea salt and freshly ground black pepper

RASPBERRY DRESSING:
2 tbsp extra virgin olive oil
2 tbsp white balsamic vinegar
100g raspberries

To make the dressing, whisk the oil and vinegar in a small bowl. Add the raspberries and whisk them in gently until roughly crushed. Season to taste.

Remove any seeds from the watermelon slices, if you prefer. Spread with half of the raspberry dressing, reserving the rest.

Arrange the tomatoes in a single layer across each watermelon slice, then cut each 'pizza' into six even-sized wedges, before placing the pieces back together in their circular shape on serving plates.

Cut each fig into six even-sized wedges and arrange one on each pizza. Crumble the feta cheese evenly over the top. Dot with the olives and drizzle with the reserved dressing. Scatter over the hazelnuts, mint and rocket, and serve at once.

FOR A TWIST...
- Meat-eaters can top their pizza with ruffles of Parma or Serrano ham.

COURGETTE 'PAPPARDELLE'

with mozzarella & minted pea pesto

Ⓥ ⒼⒻ

Thinly sliced courgette strips replace the traditional pasta pappardelle in this recipe, which is intended to be eaten at room temperature, not unlike a salad. The courgettes are slathered in a fresh, light and flavoursome pea and mint pesto, which also works perfectly as a dip or spread. This dish takes literally minutes to make, with only a handful of ingredients and of course no conventional cooking, leaving you with no excuse for not making a fresh, tasty and healthy meal any night of the week.

SERVES 4

2 large courgettes
125g ball of mozzarella
1 red chilli, finely chopped, de-seeded if you prefer less heat (optional)
25g vegetarian hard cheese, shaved
Sea salt and freshly ground black pepper

PEA PESTO:

200g frozen peas, thawed
25g toasted pine nuts or roasted hazelnuts (whole or chopped)
6 tbsp extra virgin olive oil
Large handful of fresh mint leaves
25g vegetarian hard cheese, finely grated
1 small garlic clove, peeled and roughly chopped

ESSENTIAL KIT:

Mini- or jug blender
Mandolin (or vegetable peeler)

To make the pea pesto, place the peas, nuts and oil in a mini or jug blender. Add half the mint leaves, the cheese and garlic. Blitz until fairly smooth and season to taste. Scoop the pesto out into a large bowl. This can be made up to two days in advance and kept covered in the fridge.

Slice the courgettes into long thin ribbons using a mandolin or vegetable peeler. Gently toss them through the pesto until they are evenly coated. Divide the courgette 'pappardelle' between serving plates.

Drain the mozzarella, tear into small pieces and scatter over the courgette, along with the remaining mint and the chilli, if using. Finish with the shaved cheese and a twist of black pepper, and serve. Once assembled, this is best eaten straight away.

FALAFEL WRAPS

with spinach pesto & pickled red cabbage

Falafel, the popular Middle Eastern blend of chickpeas and spices, are usually deep-fried but this recipe proves they taste just as good without frying, not to mention being healthier. Instead, they are coated in dukkah, an Egyptian spice, nut and seed mix, which gives them a wonderfully fragrant crunchy crust. You can easily make dukkah yourself, or pre-mixed tubs of it are available in delis and supermarkets. If you don't wish to pickle your own red cabbage, a shop-bought jar will be fine.

SERVES 4

FALAFEL:

50g oats

1 x 400g can chickpeas

100g sun-dried tomatoes (from a jar)

2 tbsp peanut or almond butter

½ tsp paprika

½ tsp ground cumin

1 spring onion, roughly chopped

1 small garlic clove, peeled and roughly chopped

Small handful of fresh coriander leaves

4 tsp dukkah

PICKLED RED CABBAGE:

50ml apple cider vinegar

Juice of 2 limes

1 garlic clove, peeled and crushed

1 red chilli, finely chopped, de-seeded if you prefer less heat (optional)

2 tbsp clear honey

¼ head of red cabbage

turn for more →

Half-fill a kettle with water and put it on to boil. Line a tray with non-stick baking paper and set aside.

First, prepare the pickled red cabbage. Pour the vinegar and lime juice into a medium bowl or resealable food bag. Add the garlic, chilli and honey. Stir everything together well or seal the bag and give it a good shake.

Remove the core from the red cabbage and discard. Very finely shred the leaves using a mandolin or sharp knife. Add to the vinegar mixture and give it a toss or shake to coat well. Cover the bowl or seal the bag and chill in the fridge for at least 1 hour, or overnight, tossing occasionally. This will keep in the vinegar solution in the fridge for up to two weeks.

To make the pesto, place the spinach in a large bowl and pour over enough just-boiled water to just cover, pressing it down with the back of a spoon. Leave for 3–4 minutes until wilted. Meanwhile, blitz the pumpkin seeds in a food processor to a fine crumb. Add the lime zest and juice, garlic and mint. Drain the wilted spinach and refresh under cold running water. Squeeze it dry in a clean, double-layered J-cloth and add to the processor. Blend the mixture until as smooth as possible. Add the yoghurt and oil and blitz again to blend. Season to taste. Transfer to a small bowl, cover and chill in the fridge until needed. This can be made a day ahead and kept in the fridge.

For the yoghurt drizzle, place the yoghurt in a small bowl, add the lime juice and 2 teaspoons of cold water and stir to loosen and combine. Cover and chill in the fridge until needed.

continued overleaf

SPINACH PESTO:

250g baby spinach
50g pumpkin seeds
Finely grated zest and
juice of 1 lime
1 garlic clove, roughly
chopped
Large handful of fresh mint
leaves
125g Greek or natural
yoghurt
1 tbsp extra virgin olive oil
Sea salt and freshly ground
black pepper

YOGHURT DRIZZLE:

25g Greek or natural
yoghurt
Juice of ½ lime

TO SERVE:

4 flatbreads or tortillas
10g sprouted peas or salad
cress
Hot chilli sauce, to taste
(optional)

ESSENTIAL KIT:

Kettle
Mandolin (or sharp knife)
Food processor
Toaster

To make the falafel, blend the oats in a food processor until really fine. Drain and rinse the chickpeas and add, along with the sun-dried tomatoes, nut butter, paprika, cumin, spring onion, garlic and fresh coriander. Blitz to give a moist but not wet mixture. Shape into 20 balls (each weighing about 20g), arranging them on the prepared tray as you go. Sprinkle the dukkah into a wide bowl or resealable food bag and add half the falafel. Give them a gentle toss or shake until all are coated and return them to the tray. Repeat with the remaining falafel. These can be made up to two days in advance and kept covered in the fridge, or they can also be frozen.

When ready to serve, fold the flatbreads into quarters and pop each one into a toaster. Toast for 1–2 minutes until beginning to colour. Carefully remove, open them out into halves and flip back to quarters the opposite way around. Pop them back into the toaster for a further 1–2 minutes. The flatbreads should be warmed through, lightly coloured and just turning crispy on the edges, but not crisp all over.

To assemble, open up the warmed flatbreads onto serving plates. Spread the spinach pesto into the centre of each. Drain the pickled red cabbage and scatter it over them. Arrange five falafel on each and drizzle with the lime yoghurt. Garnish with the sprouted peas or cress, and serve with hot chilli sauce for an added kick, if you like.

FOR A TWIST...
- To make these gluten-free, choose suitable oats and serve with gluten-free flatbreads or tortillas.

STUFFED MARINATED COURGETTES
with oozing cheese

Marinated courgettes are perfect for hollowing out and stuffing with a tasty filling. For an oozing topping without direct heat, use a ripened soft cheese such as Brie, Camembert or Epoisses, removed from the fridge at least 2 hours before serving. Use any leftover marinade to dress salad.

SERVES 4

200ml extra virgin olive oil
4 tbsp white wine vinegar
2 lemons
2 shallots, peeled and
finely chopped
4 garlic cloves, peeled and
finely chopped
Small handful of fresh
basil leaves, torn
1 tsp sea salt
4 small courgettes
Sea salt and freshly ground
black pepper

FILLING:
150g ripe soft cheese, such
as Brie, Camembert or
Epoisses
100g couscous
Vegetable stock cube,
powder or concentrate
(enough for 125ml)
1 x 200g can chickpeas
Handful of fresh basil leaves
25g sultanas
50g toasted flaked almonds
or pine nuts
3 tbsp sun-dried tomato
pesto

ESSENTIAL KIT:
Kettle

Pour the olive oil and vinegar into a large bowl or resealable bag. Peel the rind from the lemons and add this too, then squeeze in the juice. Add the shallots, garlic, basil and a teaspoon of salt, then mix well, or seal the bag and give it a good shake.

Halve the courgettes lengthways. Using a small teaspoon, scoop out and discard the seeded core, leaving the 'walls' about 5mm thick. Pop the courgettes in the bowl or bag, and stir or shake well to coat. Chill in the fridge for at least 4 hours or overnight, until soft. This can be done up to two days ahead.

About 2 hours before serving, remove the cheese from the fridge. Leave it in its wrapper to come to room temperature.

Half-fill the kettle and put it on to boil. When the courgettes are soft, drain them in a colander set over a large bowl to catch the marinade. Discard the lemon rind but leave everything else scattered over the courgettes. Reserve the marinade. Arrange two courgette halves, cut side up, on each serving plate.

Put the couscous in a medium bowl with some salt and pepper. Make up the stock with 125ml of just-boiled water and pour it over the couscous. Immediately cover and set aside for 5 minutes until the liquid has been absorbed and the couscous is tender.

Meanwhile, drain and rinse the chickpeas and finely shred two-thirds of the basil. When the couscous is ready, fluff it up with a fork. Add the chickpeas, shredded basil, sultanas and half the almonds or pine nuts. Drizzle with 2 tablespoons of the reserved marinade and toss everything until well mixed. Season to taste and then spoon it out evenly into the courgette halves.

Spoon the pesto into a small bowl and stir in 4 tablespoons of marinade to loosen it. Spoon a little over each courgette. Thinly slice the cheese or scoop with two teaspoons if it's too soft to cut, and arrange on top of the pesto. Scatter the stuffed courgettes with the remaining nuts and basil leaves, and serve.

SPRING VEG RISOTTO
of broccoli rice

(V) (GF)

In this alternative risotto, finely blitzed broccoli replaces the usual risotto rice, making for a healthy, low-carb, no-cook meal that's crammed with nutrient-rich green vegetables. Versatile and tasty, this is perfect for lunch, a dinner party or even a picnic. Be sure to start with your vegetables at room temperature, as they won't blanch properly if fridge-cold. Another use for the broccoli rice is to mix it with just the avocado sauce to make a delicious textured dip.

SERVES 4

4 asparagus spears (at room temperature)
75g fine green beans, trimmed (at room temperature)
100g frozen peas (thawed)
1 large head of broccoli (about 500g)
2 ripe avocados
1 garlic clove, peeled and roughly chopped
2 tbsp extra virgin olive oil
Juice of 1 lemon
Juice of 1 lime
Large handful of fresh basil leaves
Large handful of baby spinach, roughly chopped
25g vegetarian hard cheese
Sea salt and freshly ground black pepper

ESSENTIAL KIT:
Kettle
Food processor

Half-fill a kettle with water and put it on to boil.

Trim the asparagus spears, cut them in half down their length and then into 2.5cm pieces. Cut the beans into 2.5cm lengths as well. Place both in a medium bowl with the peas and a little salt. Pour enough just-boiled water over to cover. Cover and set aside for about 10 minutes until al dente.

Roughly chop the broccoli florets and stalk and give them a good rinse, draining really well. Pop them into a food processor and blitz until fairly finely chopped to look like rice. Tip into a large bowl and set aside. Wipe out the processor bowl and blade.

To make the sauce, halve the avocados, discard the stone and skin, and scoop the flesh into the processor. Add the garlic, oil, lemon and lime juice. Reserve about half the basil leaves, and add the rest. Blend to give a smooth, thick and creamy consistency. Season to taste.

Once al dente, drain the asparagus, beans and peas, refresh in ice cold water and drain again. Then throw them in on top of the broccoli and add the avocado sauce and spinach. Mix everything together really well and season to taste. This is best eaten on the day and served at room temperature.

Spoon into serving bowls, shave or finely grate the cheese on top, scatter with the reserved basil and serve.

FOR A TWIST...
- Keep the meat-eaters happy and crumble some crispy bacon strips or tear some cooked chicken or turkey over the top.

RICOTTA & ALMOND COURGETTE RAVIOLI
with crushed tomato sauce

(V) (GF)

Because this easy no-cook version of ravioli is made from courgettes, it is gluten-free as well as very low-carb. Yellow courgettes are ideal if you want your ravioli to resemble the real thing, but regular green courgettes work perfectly well. It is important to make the courgette strips as thin as possible so that they stay in shape when folded. You can use ground almonds in the filling if you prefer, but it really is worth going to the effort of blitzing toasted flaked almonds for the extra flavour they bring to the dish.

SERVES 4

2 large courgettes,
   preferably yellow
25ml extra virgin olive oil
100g toasted flaked almonds
250g ricotta
50g vegetarian cheese,
   finely grated
Small handful of fresh
   basil leaves, finely sliced
75g wild rocket
Sea salt and finely ground
   black pepper

TOMATO SALSA:

3 tbsp extra virgin olive oil
1 tsp red wine vinegar
1 shallot, peeled
1 garlic clove, peeled
300g vine-ripened cherry
   tomatoes, quartered
Large handful of fresh
   basil leaves, finely sliced

ESSENTIAL KIT:

Mandolin (or vegetable
   peeler)
Potato masher
Mini-blender

Slice the courgettes into long thin ribbons using a mandolin or vegetable peeler. You need 40 strips in total, at least 12.5cm long. Any trimmings can be used in a stir-fry, soup or salad. Toss the ribbons in a bowl with the oil until evenly coated, and set aside to soften while you prepare everything else.

For the salsa, place the oil and vinegar in a medium bowl. Finely chop the shallot and garlic, add to the bowl and whisk everything together. Season to taste, then toss the cherry tomatoes through. Using a potato masher, roughly mash them up a little so the juices squish out, making a sauce but leaving lots of texture. Finally, stir in the basil. Set aside while you prepare the filling.

Blitz 75g of the flaked almonds in a mini-blender to give fine crumbs. Tip into a medium bowl and add the ricotta, hard cheese and basil. Stir together well and season to taste. This can be made up to two days ahead.

Lay two pieces of courgette criss-crossed over each other on a clean board. Spoon a tablespoon (about 15g) of the ricotta mixture in the centre. Wrap the two ends of the bottom piece of courgette over the filling, followed by the other two ends to enclose. Turn the parcel over so it is seam-side down. Repeat to make 20 in total, arranging 5 on each serving plate as you go. If making in advance, place them on a large tray lined with non-stick baking paper. These can be made up to two days ahead.

When ready to serve, spoon the tomato salsa over the 'ravioli'. Pile some rocket leaves on top, scatter with the remaining toasted flaked almonds and finish with a twist of pepper.

BEETROOT & BEAN SLIDERS

with sugar snap 'chips' & minted salt

(V)

These fun, meat-free sliders will have everyone intrigued as they realise the burger and chips in front of them are not quite what they seem. They are super-cute as party food, but also quick and easy enough for a week-night meal. The sprinkling of minty sea salt turns sugar snap peas into something rather special. If you want to reproduce the crust on a burger that normally comes from frying, you can coat the patties in toasted sesame seeds – black, white or an attractive mix – to give a nice crunch.

MAKES 12

2 x 400g can cannellini beans
2 spring onions, finely chopped
Small handful of fresh chives, finely chopped
1 garlic clove, peeled and crushed
100g fresh white breadcrumbs
2 tsp ground cumin
200g cooked beetroot (drained weight, from a vacuum pack, not in vinegar), roughly grated
Sea salt and freshly ground black pepper

TO SERVE:

200g cottage cheese
1 tbsp prepared horseradish sauce
12 mini burger buns
15g sprouted peas or salad cress
1 large Granny Smith apple

turn for more ➜

Put the kettle on to boil, about a quarter full. Line a tray with non-stick baking paper and set aside.

Place the cottage cheese and horseradish in a mini-blender, blitz until smooth and pop into a small bowl. Alternatively, for a chunkier texture, simply mix them together in a small bowl. Season to taste. Cover and chill in the fridge until ready to serve.

Place the sugar snaps in a small bowl and pour over enough just-boiled water to cover. Cover and set aside for about 10 minutes until al dente. Grind the salt and mint together in a pestle and mortar until well combined. Alternatively, blitz them together briefly in a mini-blender or coffee grinder. Tip into a small bowl, cover and chill in the fridge until ready to serve.

Next, prepare the sliders. Drain and rinse the cannellini beans and roughly mash them in a large bowl. Add the spring onions, chopped chives, garlic, breadcrumbs and cumin. Squeeze the beetroot in a clean, double-layered J-cloth until it is really dry, catching the juices in a bowl. Add the beetroot to the bean mixture along with 2 tablespoons of the beetroot juice, and mix everything together really well. Season to taste.

Shape into 12 small even-sized burger patties, 6cm wide and 2cm deep (about 65g each), arranging them on the prepared tray as you go. These can be made up to two days in advance and kept covered in the fridge, or they can also be frozen.

Drain the sugar snaps, arrange in serving bowls or small glasses and sprinkle with the mint salt.

continued overleaf

SUGAR SNAP 'CHIPS':

300g sugar snaps (at room temperature)
1 tbsp flaked sea salt
1 tbsp roughly chopped fresh mint

ESSENTIAL KIT:

Kettle
Mini-blender, coffee grinder or pestle and mortar
Toaster
Mandolin (or sharp knife)

Split the burger buns in half and toast in a toaster until golden. Pile some sprouts or cress on the base of each bun and sit a burger on top.

Very finely slice the apple using a mandolin or sharp knife, into 24 slices, removing any pips as you go. Arrange a couple of apple slices on top of each burger and spoon a little cottage cheese sauce on top. Top with the bun lid, and serve with the sugar snaps and any remaining cottage cheese sauce on the side.

FOR A TWIST...

- Shape the burger mix into four regular-sized patties, if you prefer, and use standard burger buns.

- For a gluten-free version, make sure to use suitable breadcrumbs and burger buns.

NO-COOK COURGETTE LASAGNE

Forget everything you know about lasagne! This no-cook twist on the classic Italian dish will challenge your preconceptions, with its layers of fresh courgette, herby soft cheese, a delicious nutty meat substitute and aromatic tomato dressing, which all come together in a refreshing symphony of flavours. Since there is no actual pasta involved, it is also an excellent gluten-free and low-carb option. Choose the straightest possible courgettes you can find, to help ensure even coverage, but don't worry if you can only get curved ones as you can always do some patchwork to fill in the gaps.

SERVES 4

2 long, straight courgettes
25ml extra virgin olive oil
**4 vine-ripened tomatoes,
    thinly sliced**
**Small handful of fresh basil
    leaves, to garnish**
**Sea salt and freshly ground
    black pepper**

CHEESE SAUCE:

400g full-fat cream cheese
75g crème fraîche
**Large handful of mixed herb
    leaves (e.g. chives, flat-
    leaf parsley, basil, mint
    or dill), finely chopped**
**1 small garlic clove, peeled
    and crushed**
**50g vegetarian hard cheese,
    finely grated**

NUTTY LAYER:

50g walnuts
50g almonds
50g pecan nuts
**100g sun-dried tomatoes
    (from a jar)**
**25g vegetarian hard cheese,
    finely grated**

turn for more →

Slice the courgettes into very thin ribbons using a mandolin or vegetable peeler. Place the ribbons in a large bowl, drizzle with the olive oil and toss until evenly coated. Set aside while you prepare the rest of the recipe.

To make the cheese sauce, beat the cream cheese and crème fraîche together in a medium bowl to loosen and blend. Add the chopped herbs and garlic. Reserve a third of the Parmesan and add the rest of it to the mixture. Stir everything together well and season to taste.

For the nutty mixture, place the nuts, sun dried-tomatoes and cheese in a food processor. Blitz until roughly chopped. Season to taste. This can be made up to three days in advance and kept covered in the fridge.

To make the tomato sauce, first rinse out the processor bowl, then add the tomatoes, tomato paste, shallot and garlic. Pour in the lemon juice, oil and mustard and give everything a good blitz until the mixture is as smooth as possible. Finally, add the basil leaves and give it another quick blitz. Season to taste. This sauce is for serving rather than for assembly, and can also be made up to three days ahead and kept in the fridge.

When you have prepared all the elements and are ready to assemble your lasagne, gradually build up layers of courgette, cheese sauce, nutty mixture and tomatoes in the baking dish, using the ingredients in any order you like, but starting and ending with a layer of the sliced courgettes. Top this with an even sprinkling of the reserved cheese.

continued overleaf

TOMATO SAUCE:

2 vine-ripened tomatoes, roughly chopped

1 tbsp sun-dried tomato paste

1 small shallot, peeled and roughly chopped

1 small garlic clove, peeled and roughly chopped

Juice of ½ lemon

50ml olive oil

1 tsp Dijon mustard

Small handful of fresh basil leaves

ESSENTIAL KIT:

Mandolin (or vegetable peeler)

Food processor

1.75-litre baking dish, 20cm square and 5cm deep

The lasagne can be served straight away or alternatively you can cover it and chill in the fridge for up to a couple of days. Allow it to return to room temperature before serving.

To serve, spoon a pool of the tomato sauce in the centre of each serving plate. Cut the lasagne into four even-sized pieces and sit each one in the centre of the sauce. Garnish with scattered basil leaves, and serve.

FOR A TWIST...

- Make your lasagne cheesier with 200g crumbled feta, goats' or blue cheese (either mixed into the cheese sauce or sprinkled on as separate layer)

- Add some crunch with a layer of finely chopped yellow pepper

- Use a drained jar of marinated mushrooms, artichokes, olives or roasted peppers for an extra layer

- Throw in a couple of handfuls of baby spinach or wild rocket

ITALIAN SLICE
with a courgette lattice top

Ⓥ ⒼⒻ

Since this beautiful loaf is made in advance and then left to set, it is perfect for a fuss-free dinner party. It is also a great item to have in the fridge for nibbling on at snack time, or for lunch. The lattice top isn't as tricky as it might look and is worth attempting for the lovely finished effect. If you can't master it, don't let that put you off – strips of courgette all laid in one direction also look charming. Most loaf tins are wider at the top, so each layer of goats' cheese requires a slightly different quantity in order for them to all end up the same thickness when turned out. However, if your mould is of uniform width all the way up then simply use 100g of goats' cheese for each layer.

SERVES 4

50ml extra virgin olive oil
Finely grated zest and juice of 1 lemon
1 garlic clove, peeled and crushed
2 small, thin courgettes
20 fine asparagus spears (about 175g, at room temperature)
400g soft, rindless goats' cheese (at room temperature)
250g roasted red peppers (from a jar)
150g pitted black olives
Sea salt and freshly ground black pepper

TO SERVE:

1 tbsp balsamic glaze
Large handful of fresh basil leaves
100g mixed salad leaves
2 tbsp toasted pine nuts

turn for more →

Put a kettle on to boil, about a quarter full.

Pour the oil into a wide, shallow dish and add the lemon zest and juice and the garlic. Season with a little salt and pepper and mix everything together well. Slice the courgettes into long thin ribbons using a mandolin or vegetable peeler. Toss through the oil mixture until well coated and leave for 15 minutes to marinate and soften.

Trim the woody ends of the asparagus until the spears are half the length of the loaf tin. Place them in a wide bowl with a little salt, and pour over enough just-boiled water to cover. Cover and leave for about 5 minutes until al dente.

Beat the goats' cheese in a medium bowl to loosen it up. Season to taste and set aside.

Dab the roasted peppers and olives with kitchen paper to soak up any excess liquid or oil. Cut the olives in half and set aside.

Drain the asparagus well, refresh in ice-cold water and drain again. Drain the courgettes over a medium bowl, allowing excess marinade to drip off and reserving it for later.

Lay out a large double layer of cling film. Arrange strips of courgette touching each other in a single layer to result in a 20 x 30cm rectangle. Weave the remaining strips across in the opposite direction, bringing them under and over the first layer to give a lattice effect. Trim as necessary to fit and neaten.

continued overleaf

8 crispbreads or slices of toasted sourdough (choose gluten-free options if necessary)

Kettle
Mandolin (or vegetable peeler)
1-litre loaf tin (10 x 20cm at the top)

Carefully lift the cling film, with the courgettes still on top, into the loaf tin, pressing it evenly into the base and edges of the tin. Leave the excess cling film and courgette ends hanging over the edge.

Spread 75g of the goats' cheese in an even layer in the bottom of the tin, being careful not to disturb the courgettes. Arrange the roasted peppers on top in an even layer, followed by 100g more goats' cheese. Next, arrange the asparagus spears lengthways in two rows and again top with 100g of goats' cheese. Sprinkle the olives on top in an even layer and finally spread with the last 125g of the cheese. Flip the excess courgette and cling film over the top and chill in the fridge for at least 8 hours or overnight, until set firm. This can be made up to two days in advance.

When ready to serve, remove the loaf from the tin by opening out the cling film and inverting the whole thing onto a long plate. Using a long, sharp knife, dipped in boiled water and wiped dry between every slice, cut it into eight even-sized pieces. Arrange two on each serving plate and drizzle balsamic glaze around them. Toss the basil and salad leaves in the reserved marinade and arrange on each plate. Scatter with pine nuts and serve with crispbreads or slices of toasted sourdough.

FOR A TWIST...

- Serve with basil pesto instead of (or in addition to) the balsamic glaze.

- Use slices of mozzarella instead of goats' cheese, if you prefer.

MIXED BEAN & TOMATO 'CASSEROLE'
with bulghur wheat

(V)

The sauce for this alternative 'casserole' is made from fresh, ripe tomatoes, naturally thickened with breadcrumbs. Bulghur wheat is a perfect grain for quick no-cook recipes as it is in fact pre-cooked so needs only a soak in hot water (or longer in cold) to make it tender. If you can't find bulghur or don't wish to use it, you can use a different grain. A huge range of pre-cooked grains are sold in packets these days, such as rice, quinoa, freekeh, spelt or mixed grains.

SERVES 4

250g bulghur wheat
500g ripe tomatoes,
    roughly chopped
3 slices of stale white bread
    or 75g panko
    breadcrumbs
1 garlic clove, peeled and
    roughly chopped
6 tbsp extra virgin olive oil
1 tbsp sherry vinegar
1 small red onion, peeled
    and very finely chopped
1 small yellow pepper,
    de-seeded and finely
    chopped
Large handful of fresh
    flat-leaf parsley leaves,
    finely chopped
Juice of 1 lemon
2 x 400g cans mixed beans,
    drained and rinsed
Sea salt and freshly ground
    black pepper

ESSENTIAL KIT:
Kettle
Jug blender

Half-fill the kettle with water and bring to the boil.

Pour the bulghur wheat into a medium bowl and stir in a little salt and pepper. Pour over 500ml of just-boiled water, cover and leave to soak for 30 minutes.

Place the tomatoes in a blender. Remove the crusts from the bread, tear up the slices and pop them (or the panko breadcrumbs) into the blender as well. Add the garlic, along with 4 tablespoons of the oil and the vinegar. Blitz for 1–2 minutes until as smooth as possible. Season to taste and set aside. This can be made up to two days in advance.

When the bulghur wheat is tender, drain it well, squeezing as much excess water out as possible. Return it to the bowl, add the remaining 2 tablespoons of oil, the onion, half the pepper, half the chopped parsley and the lemon juice. Toss well together and season to taste.

Divide the bulghur wheat evenly between serving plates. Spoon the tomato sauce on top and scatter with beans. Sprinkle with the remaining yellow pepper and parsley, and serve.

FOR A TWIST...
- Use couscous for an even speedier meal – it 'cooks' in the same way as the bulghur wheat but only takes 5 minutes.
- To make this gluten-free, swap the bulghur wheat for pre-cooked quinoa (no need to soak) and use gluten-free breadcrumbs in the sauce.

FISH DISHES

'SEARED' TUNA STEAK
with quinoa salad & ginger-pickled cucumber

While the tuna in this dish is not cooked in the normal sense, it is cured in an acidic marinade, and it is this process that gives it a 'seared' look. Be sure to buy very fresh fish. Usually, if you marinate a fish before cooking it, you shouldn't eat the marinade without cooking it too, but here it's fine to use as a dressing because of the curing. If using a food bag, sit it in a jug or bowl when filling to prevent spilling. If you can't find toasted sesame seeds, use regular ones.

SERVES 2

5cm piece of fresh ginger
Juice of 1 lemon
100ml light soy sauce
50ml mirin
Large handful of fresh coriander, finely chopped
2 x 125g very fresh tuna steaks
½ cucumber
2 tbsp pickled ginger
4 tbsp pickled ginger juice
1 tbsp pink peppercorns
1 tsp black peppercorns
½ tsp toasted sesame seeds

QUINOA SALAD:

250g pouch of cooked quinoa
½ small red onion, peeled and very finely chopped
1 red chilli, finely chopped, de-seeded if you prefer less heat (optional)
Large handful of fresh coriander leaves

ESSENTIAL KIT:

Mandolin, julienne peeler or sharp knife
Pestle and mortar, or heavy-based pan

Peel and very finely chop the ginger and place in a small bowl or resealable food bag. Add the lemon juice, soy sauce, mirin and chopped coriander, and mix everything together well. Slide the tuna steaks into the mixture, tossing to coat. Cover or seal and pop in the fridge to marinate for at least 2 hours or overnight.

When almost ready to serve, halve the cucumber lengthways and remove the seeded core using a teaspoon. Shred the flesh into long thin strips with a mandolin, julienne peeler or sharp knife. Toss in a small bowl with the pickled ginger and its juice. Set aside until ready to serve.

Crush the pink and black peppercorns in a pestle and mortar or on a chopping board with the bottom of a heavy based pan. Scatter them over a large plate and set aside.

Place the quinoa, onion and chilli (if using) into a large bowl. Reserve a small handful of the coriander, finely chop the rest and add. Add 4 tablespoons of the tuna marinade to the bowl and toss everything together.

Divide the quinoa salad between serving plates. Remove the tuna from the marinade and press each side of the steaks into the crushed peppercorns to coat evenly. Lay a steak on each bed of quinoa. Drizzle with a couple of spoonfuls of the marinade and pour the rest into a serving jug. Spoon the ginger-pickled cucumber onto the plate. Sprinkle with sesame seeds and the reserved coriander, and serve.

FOR A TWIST...
● To make this gluten-free, use tamari instead of soy sauce.

DIY SUSHI CONES

with pickled radishes & miso mayonnaise

(GF)

A platter of sushi ingredients is a fun way to share a meal with friends and family. Guests can choose their fillings and hand-roll their cones, known in Japan as temaki. Kids love the novelty of assembling their own supper, so this is a great way to introduce them to sushi.

SERVES 4 (MAKES 12 CONES)

2 spring onions
2 x 250g pouches of cooked
    basmati rice
200g hot-smoked salmon
24 cooked, peeled prawns
2 tbsp fish roe
½ ripe mango
¼ cucumber
1 avocado
Juice of ½ lime
25g sprouted peas or
    salad cress
4 tsp rice vinegar
100g mayonnaise
1 tbsp white miso paste
1 tbsp wasabi paste
6 nori seaweed sheets
¼ tsp toasted black sesame
    seeds (optional)
Small handful of fresh
    coriander leaves
Sea salt

PICKLED RADISH:

Juice of ½ lime
1 tbsp rice vinegar
1 tsp caster sugar
4 radishes, finely sliced

ESSENTIAL KIT:

Kettle
Mini-blender

Half-fill a kettle with water and put it on to boil.

Halve the spring onions across the width and slice into long, very thin matchsticks. Submerge in a small bowl of iced water and chill in the fridge until needed.

To pickle the radish, pour the lime juice into a small bowl or resealable food bag. Add the vinegar and sugar, and whisk or shake until the sugar dissolves. Toss the radishes in the liquid and set aside to pickle, tossing occasionally. This can be prepared up to a day in advance.

Place the rice in a small bowl and pour over enough just-boiled water to cover. Cover and set aside for 5 minutes.

Flake the salmon into pieces and arrange on a large serving platter with the prawns. Spoon the fish roe into a small bowl and add it to the platter. Peel and de-stone the mango and slice the flesh thinly. Using a vegetable peeler, shave the cucumber into thin ribbons. Quarter the avocado, discard the skin and stone, and slice each piece. Squeeze the lime juice over to prevent discoloration. Arrange the mango, cucumber, avocado and a pile of sprouted peas or salad cress on the platter.

Drain the rice well and blitz in a mini-blender until finely chopped. It should be sticky when squeezed. Drizzle with the vinegar, scatter with a little salt and toss until evenly coated. Spoon into a small bowl.

Stir together the mayonnaise and miso paste in a small bowl. Squeeze the wasabi paste into another small bowl. Cut the nori seaweed sheets in half and lay on a separate serving plate (being careful not to get them wet).

continued overleaf

Drain the radishes and place in a small bowl on the platter. The spring onions should have curled by now, so drain them well and pile them up on the platter as well. If using, scatter the black sesame seeds over the mango and rice. Finally, garnish the whole platter with the coriander leaves, and serve.

To assemble the rolls, spread rice in a thin even layer on a piece of seaweed. Then with it in your hand, roll it up to form a cone shape. The rice should be moist and sticky enough to hold the cone shape in place. Then simply fill the cone with your choice of fillings, a dot of wasabi and a drizzle of the miso mayo, and enjoy.

FOR A TWIST...

- Instead of nori seaweed sheets, use soy wrappers in the same way. They can be found in Asian stores and come in different colours, some speckled with sesame seeds.

BUTTERNUT SQUASH 'SPAGHETTI'
with clams & sun-dried tomato sauce

(GF)

Spaghetti alle vongole, or spaghetti with clams, is an Italian classic. The dish is usually made with fresh seafood, but jars of clams are handy to have in the store cupboard and work just as well. You might not have known you can eat butternut squash raw but it is lovely, moist and sweet if spiralised or finely shredded. Serve this dish for a romantic meal or a healthy suppertime treat.

SERVES 2
175g semi-dried tomatoes (drained weight)
2 garlic cloves, peeled and roughly chopped
1 red chilli, roughly chopped (de-seeded if you prefer less heat)
Large handful of fresh basil leaves
1 medium butternut squash
1 x 200g jar clams, drained and well rinsed
Sea salt and freshly ground black pepper

ESSENTIAL KIT:
Mini-blender
Spiraliser, mandolin or julienne/vegetable peeler

Place the tomatoes, garlic, chilli and half the basil leaves in a mini-blender. Blitz to a rough purée. Season to taste and pour into a large bowl. This can be made up to three days in advance and kept covered in the fridge.

Peel the squash and discard the seeds. If using a spiraliser, mandolin or julienne peeler, you will likely have to cut the squash lengthways into quarters in order to be able to shred it properly. Shred it to form long, thin 'spaghetti'. Alternatively, use a vegetable peeler to slice it into thin ribbons more like pappardelle. Either way, add it to the sauce, with the clams, and toss until well coated.

Pile a serving into the centre of each plate. Scatter with the remaining basil, and serve.

FOR A TWIST...
- Replace the clams with pre-cooked chicken pieces or – for a vegetarian version – with ready-to-eat beans or crumbled goats' cheese.

HOT-SMOKED SALMON BURGER
with pineapple salsa & avocado 'chips'

Hot-smoked salmon makes a very tasty burger, especially when combined with this sweet pineapple salsa (or papaya also works nicely). The avocado 'chips' are a clever and healthy alternative to their usual fried friend, with a lovely crunchy coating of toasted nutty crumbs.

SERVES 4

1 small red onion, peeled
400g hot-smoked salmon
2 tsp Dijon mustard
1 red chilli, finely chopped, de-seeded if you prefer less heat (optional)
Large handful of fresh coriander leaves, finely chopped, plus extra to serve
4 ciabatta or burger buns
4 tbsp mayonnaise
Big handful of wild rocket
Sea salt and freshly ground black pepper

PINEAPPLE SALSA:

¼ pineapple
¼ cucumber, very finely chopped
Finely grated zest and juice of ½ lime

AVOCADO CHIPS:

50g toasted flaked almonds
15g Parmesan, finely grated
¼ tsp paprika
2 ripe avocados

ESSENTIAL KIT:

Kettle
Mini-blender

Put the kettle on to boil, about a quarter full.

Very finely chop the red onion and place in a small bowl. Pour over enough just-boiled water to cover. Leave aside to soak for about 5 minutes, until softened in texture and taste.

Meanwhile, flake the salmon into a large bowl, discarding any skin, bones or brown residue. Place half the salmon in a mini-blender and blitz until fine (it should be like a paste when squashed together). Return this to the flaked salmon and add the mustard, chilli (if using) and chopped coriander. Drain the red onion well, squeeze it dry and add this too. Mix everything together well and season to taste (you may only need pepper).

Shape into four burger patties (just over 100g each) and arrange on a plate or small tray lined with non-stick baking paper. While not necessary, these can be chilled in the fridge for at least 1 hour to firm them up a little more. They can be made up to one day in advance or longer if frozen.

Make the salsa just before serving. Peel and core the pineapple, very finely chop the flesh and pop in a medium bowl. Add the cucumber, lime zest and juice, and toss gently. Season to taste.

Finally, for the avocado chips, blitz the flaked almonds in a mini- blender until finely chopped. Tip into a wide, shallow bowl and add the Parmesan and paprika. Stir together and season a little. Quarter the avocados and discard their stones and skin. Cut each quarter in half lengthways, giving 16 pieces in total. Carefully toss the avocado 'chips' through the nutty cheese mixture until evenly coated, arranging them on a tray lined with non-stick baking paper as you go.

To serve, spread each roll or bun base with mayonnaise and scatter with rocket. Sit a salmon burger on top, spoon over some salsa and garnish with coriander. Add the bread lid, arrange four avocado 'chips' beside each one and serve at once.

EASY-PEASY PAELLA

This quick and easy no-cook paella will have you fooled into thinking you are basking in Spanish sunshine. It is packed full of flavours, from saffron to smoked paprika, and brimming with seafood, chicken and chorizo, all of which can be bought ready-cooked from the supermarket and added to this dish for a fabulous shortcut supper.

SERVES 4

2 x 250g pouches of cooked long-grain rice
100g cooked chicken, diced
8 cooked chorizo slices, cut into 5mm-wide matchsticks
3 spring onions, sliced
100g roasted red peppers (from a jar), thinly sliced
Large handful of fresh flat-leaf parsley leaves, roughly chopped
200g pre-cooked seafood mix, thawed if frozen
50g frozen peas, thawed
1 lemon
Sea salt and freshly ground black pepper

DRESSING:

2 pinches of saffron
Juice of 1 lemon
1 tsp tomato or sun-dried tomato purée
¼ tsp cayenne pepper or smoked paprika
1 garlic clove, peeled and crushed

ESSENTIAL KIT:

Kettle

Half-fill the kettle with water and put it on to boil.

Place the saffron for the dressing in a large bowl, pour over 2 tablespoons of just-boiled water and leave to infuse for 5 minutes.

Pour the rice into a small bowl and pour over enough just-boiled water to cover. Cover and set aside for 5 minutes.

Once the saffron has soaked, add the lemon juice, tomato purée, cayenne or paprika and the garlic, and stir everything together.

Drain the rice well, refreshing it under cold water if you don't wish to eat it warm or are preparing the dish in advance. Add the rice to the dressing, stirring it thoroughly until evenly coated. Then add the prepared meat and vegetables. Reserve half the parsley for serving, and add the rest, along with the seafood mix and peas. Toss everything together until well mixed. Season to taste.

Spoon onto serving plates and sprinkle with the reserved parsley. Cut the lemon into four wedges and serve one on each plate. Alternatively, present in a paella pan at the table and everyone can help themselves.

GRAVADLAX SALMON

with noodles, hot-and-sour cucumber & wasabi peas

Gravadlax is a dish of salmon cold-cured in salt, sugar and flavourings (traditionally dill) over a few days. Weighing down the fish is important so as to extract liquid (which the salt and sugar then absorb). This is very much worth the wait, particularly when served with hot and sour cucumber and other tasty trimmings. It makes an impressive course for a dinner party or family lunch. If you can't find toasted sesame seeds, just use regular ones.

SERVES 6–8

500g rock salt

225g caster sugar

4 lemongrass sticks, thinly sliced

2 red chillies, thinly sliced

20cm length of very fresh salmon fillet from the thick end (about 800g), skin on, trimmed, pin-boned and scaled

2 thumb-sized pieces of fresh ginger, peeled and finely grated

500g thin rice noodles

50g wasabi peas, roughly chopped

2 tbsp crispy onions (optional)

Small handful of fresh coriander leaves

HOT-AND-SOUR CUCUMBER:

Juice of 2 limes

100ml rice wine vinegar

2 tbsp clear honey

4 tsp toasted sesame seeds

1 tsp dried chilli flakes

1 cucumber

turn for more →

Toss the salt, sugar, lemongrass and chilli together in a medium bowl. Lay a double layer of cling film, large enough to completely wrap around the piece of fish, on a work surface. Spread half the salt mixture in the centre and sit the salmon fillet on top, skin-side down. Massage the grated ginger into the flesh all over the top, then sprinkle evenly with the remaining salt mixture.

Wrap the cling film around to enclose the salmon tightly and place in a deep-sided dish or tray. Top with a smaller tray or plate and weigh down with heavy objects like full cans of food. Place in the fridge and leave to cure for at least 24 hours and up to 48 hours. Turn the salmon parcel over every 12 hours or so.

For the hot and sour cucumber, pour the lime juice into a medium bowl. Add the vinegar, honey, sesame seeds and chilli flakes, and stir together well. Halve the cucumber lengthways, de-seed with a teaspoon and cut into 5mm slices. Toss in the dressing and set aside until needed. This can be prepared up to a week in advance and kept in the fridge.

When almost ready to serve, fill the kettle with water and put it on to boil.

Lay the noodles in a wide dish and pour over enough just-boiled water to cover. Cover and leave to soak for 8–10 minutes (or according to the packet instructions) until tender, stirring halfway through.

Remove the cling film from the salmon. Using kitchen paper, wipe off the salt mixture and any juices. Slice thinly with a long sharp knife, leaving the skin behind.

continued overleaf

**Deep-sided baking dish or
non-metallic tray**
**Smaller tray or plate to fit
inside**
**About 4 heavy objects like
full food cans**
Kettle

When the noodles are tender, drain them well. They are delicious served warm with the salmon, or can be rinsed under cold running water if you would prefer them cool. Arrange them on a long serving platter and top with the salmon slices in an overlapping row.

Spoon some of the cucumber down the centre, drizzle with some of the dressing and serve the remaining cucumber and dressing in a small bowl. Sprinkle with some of the wasabi peas, serving the remainder in a small bowl. Garnish with the crispy onions, if using, and finish with scattered coriander leaves. Arrange everything on the table for everyone to help themselves.

FOR A TWIST...

- Omit the crispy onions and wasabi peas to make this gluten-free. Serve with cashew nuts instead.

- Serve on toasts as canapés, with or without cream cheese or a salmon mousse (see page 69).

- Use capers instead of wasabi peas.

- Replace the coriander with dill, which also works well with salmon.

FRESH TUNA TARTARE
with wasabi papaya slaw

Tartare is typically a raw dish, but this recipe includes lime juice to 'cook' or cure the tuna, which gives it a particularly zingy tastiness. The wasabi mayonnaise in the slaw adds a wonderful kick to this dish, beautifully marrying the zesty tuna and sweet papaya. It is important not to mix the slaw ingredients together until just before serving or it may become soggy. If you can't find toasted sesame seeds, just use regular ones.

SERVES 2

250g very fresh tuna fillet
Thumb-sized piece of fresh ginger, peeled and very finely grated
Very finely grated zest and juice of ½ lime
4 fresh chives, finely chopped
2 tsp fish sauce
2 tsp light soy sauce
1 tsp toasted sesame seeds
2 small radishes, very finely sliced

PAPAYA SLAW:
50g mayonnaise
1 tsp wasabi paste
Juice of ½ lime
1 small papaya (about 500g)
½ cucumber
¼ iceberg lettuce
Small handful of fresh coriander leaves
Sesame crispbreads, breadsticks or Asian crisps, to serve

ESSENTIAL KIT:
Mandolin or julienne peeler (or sharp knife)
2 x 175ml serving glasses

Wrap the tuna in cling film and place it in the freezer for 30 minutes to 1 hour until firm. This chills the fish so it is less wobbly when dicing finely. Make sure you don't leave it any longer or it will begin to actually freeze.

For the slaw, place the mayonnaise and wasabi in a large bowl with the lime juice, and whisk until blended. Peel and de-seed the papaya and chop into small dice. Slice the cucumber into long thin 'spaghetti' with a mandolin, julienne peeler or sharp knife. Very finely shred the lettuce. Reserve a third of the coriander leaves for garnishing and roughly chop the rest. Set everything aside for mixing just before serving.

Once firm, slice the tuna into strips and then into 1cm cubes and place in a medium bowl. Add the ginger, lime zest and juice, chives, fish sauce, soy sauce and sesame seeds, and stir well.

When ready to serve, add all of the slaw ingredients to the mayonnaise and gently toss together to coat. Spoon this into the bottoms of the serving glasses. Divide the tuna tartare evenly between them. Arrange the radishes in a neat stack on top. Decorate with the reserved coriander, and serve at once with sesame crispbreads, breadsticks or Asian crisps.

FOR A TWIST...
• If you want to make this gluten-free, choose suitable crispbreads and a gluten-free wasabi paste, and use tamari instead of soy sauce.

PRAWN, SMOKED SALMON & CRAB TERRINE
with lemony leaves

Elegant and delicious, this mousse-like seafood terrine is topped with a beautiful pattern of prawns. It looks very impressive but is surprisingly easy to achieve. It is important to chill the terrine well to give a firm set, which will allow for neat slices on serving. Be sure to squeeze any excess water from the crabmeat. It might take a pack of about 150g of crabmeat to give 100g when squeezed dry.

SERVES 6

3 gelatine leaves
Sunflower oil, for greasing
12 small cooked, peeled
    tiger prawns (about 75g)
400g smoked salmon
25g unsalted butter,
    softened
150ml double cream
1 tbsp brandy (optional)
Few dashes of Worcester
    sauce
Few dashes of hot pepper
    sauce (such as Tabasco)
100g dry, white crabmeat
    (see introduction above)
Sea salt and freshly ground
    black pepper

LEMONY SALAD:

4 tbsp extra virgin olive oil
Juice of ½ lemon
1 tsp Dijon mustard
¼ tsp clear honey
    (optional)
125g mixed salad leaves

turn for more ➜

Place the gelatine leaves in a small, wide bowl, pour over enough cold water to cover and leave to soak for about 10 minutes until they are softened.

Put the kettle on to boil, about a quarter full.

Grease the loaf tin with oil and line with non-stick baking paper, leaving a 5cm excess hanging over the edges. Cut the prawns in half horizontally down their length. Lay them out in neat rows, pink-side down, on the bottom of the tin. Pack them in tightly against each other to keep gaps to a minimum. Chill in the fridge.

Place the smoked salmon and butter in a food processor and blend until smooth. Drain the water from the softened gelatine, pop it back in the bowl and pour over 1 tablespoon of just-boiled water, stirring until dissolved. Pour this into the processor and add the cream and brandy (if using). Blend until well combined and then add Worcester sauce, hot pepper sauce and seasoning to taste (remembering the smoked salmon may be salty). Transfer to a medium bowl and stir in three-quarters of the crabmeat.

Spoon the mixture into the tin and spread evenly, being careful not to disturb the prawns. Cover and chill in the fridge for at least 6 hours or overnight, until set.

To prepare the salad dressing, put the oil, lemon juice and mustard into a large bowl, whisk together and season to taste, adding the honey for a little sweetness if you like. Toss the salad leaves through the dressing when ready to serve.

Invert the loaf tin onto a long serving platter to reveal the

continued overleaf

**Small handful of fresh
dill leaves**
**1 chive flower, broken up
(optional)**
1 lemon
**Crispbreads, crackers or
wholemeal bread slices
(choose gluten-free
options if necessary)**

Kettle
1-litre loaf tin (10 x 20cm)
Food processor

terrine. Scatter the reserved crab meat over the top, and garnish with the dill and chive flower. Cut the lemon into six wedges and pop in a small bowl.

Place the terrine on the table with the dressed salad, lemon wedges and crispbreads, crackers or slices of bread. To serve, use a long, sharp knife to cut the terrine into 12 slices, dipping the knife in hot water and wiping dry before each cut for a cleaner and easier result.

FOR A TWIST...

- Serve in individual portions – spoon the seafood mixture into 6 x 125ml ramekins or glasses and arrange the prawns on top.

SMOKED MACKEREL PÂTÉ POTS
with lemony asparagus salad

GF

This is probably the easiest pâté you will ever make. It is very moreish, so serve with plenty of crispbreads or crackers for feasting. The pots are great for taking on a picnic, a day out or trip to the beach. Packets of smoked mackerel often come with a flavouring such as lemon or black pepper; choose your favourite variety for this dish.

SERVES 4

500g smoked mackerel fillets

2 spring onions, finely chopped

1 celery stick, finely chopped

250g full-fat cream cheese

Juice of 1 lemon

Small handful of fresh dill leaves, roughly chopped

Sea salt and freshly ground black pepper

ASPARAGUS SALAD:

Finely grated zest and juice of 1 lemon

2 tbsp olive oil

2 tsp clear honey

12 asparagus spears

TO SERVE:

Small handful of fresh dill or celery leaves

Crispbreads or wholemeal crackers (choose gluten-free options if necessary)

Remove the skin and any dark residue from the mackerel fillets and flake the flesh into a medium bowl. Add the spring onions, celery, cream cheese, lemon juice and dill. Mix everything together well and season to taste (it may not need salt). This can be served straight away or cover and chill in the fridge until needed. This will keep for up to a few days in the fridge.

To make the salad dressing, place the lemon zest and juice into a medium bowl. Add the oil and honey and give it a good whisk, until well blended. Season to taste and set aside.

Snap any woody ends from the asparagus. Using a vegetable peeler, carefully shave the asparagus spears into long thin ribbons. Just before serving, toss them through the dressing until evenly coated.

To serve the mackerel pâté, divide it evenly between small serving bowls, glasses or jars and garnish with dill sprigs or celery leaves. Place on a serving plate or board. Arrange the shaved asparagus salad beside it and serve with crispbreads.

MEDITERRANEAN TUNA CROQUETTES
with fennel citrus salad & dill cream

GF

Potato croquettes are given a new lease of life in this dish, with its Mediterranean flavours and accompanying fresh, zesty salad. It is best to coat the croquettes in crumbs just before serving so they remain crunchy, or just a short while in advance if need be. Use crushed croutons, crackers or even cornflakes to coat them instead of vegetable crisps, if you prefer.

SERVES 4

1 x 400g can tuna in
    sunflower oil
400g cooked, mashed
    potato
1 small red onion, peeled
    and very finely chopped
1 small garlic clove, peeled
    and very finely chopped
1 small red chilli, finely
    chopped, de-seeded
    if you prefer less heat
    (optional)
10 black olives, pitted and
    roughly chopped
2 tbsp capers, roughly
    chopped
Small handful of fresh
    flat-leaf parsley or basil
    leaves, finely chopped
150g vegetable crisps
Sea salt and freshly ground
    black pepper

DILL CREAM:

125g sour cream
1 tbsp wholegrain mustard
Juice of ½ lemon
Small handful of fresh dill
    leaves, finely chopped

turn for more →

Line a tray with non-stick baking paper and set aside.

To make the croquettes, drain the tuna well and place in a large bowl along with the mashed potato. Add all the other ingredients, except the crisps, and stir everything together until well blended. Season to taste.

Divide the mixture into 12 even-sized pieces (weighing about 50g each). Using clean hands, shape each one into a neat sausage shape with pointed ends. Arrange, spaced apart, on the tray as you go. Cover and chill in the fridge for at least 1 hour or overnight, until firm. These can be made up to two days in advance.

To make the sauce, spoon the sour cream and mustard into a screw-top jar. Add the lemon juice and chopped dill. Secure the lid and shake until well blended. Season to taste and chill in the fridge until ready to serve.

To prepare the salad, use a small, sharp knife to cut the peel and pith from the oranges and pink grapefruit. Cut the pink grapefruit into thin slices and place in a small bowl. Then remove the segments of the oranges from between their membranes, allowing them and any juices to drop into the same small bowl as you go. Drain any caught juices off into a medium bowl, and add any remaining juice squeezed out of the membranes to it.

Add the olive oil, lemon juice and honey to the orange juice. Whisk until blended, season to taste and set aside.

continued overleaf

CITRUS SALAD:

2 oranges
1 pink grapefruit
6 tbsp extra virgin olive oil
Juice of 1 lemon
1 tsp clear honey
1 small fennel bulb
16 black olives

ESSENTIAL KIT:

Mini-blender or resealable
food bag and rolling pin
Mandolin (or sharp knife)

When ready to serve, blitz the vegetable crisps in a mini-blender until fine. Alternatively, seal them in a food bag and bash with a rolling pin. Tip the crumbs into a wide, shallow bowl. Working with one at a time, gently roll the croquettes in the crumbs until evenly coated all over. Return to the tray as you go.

Very thinly slice the fennel (reserving any fronds) using a mandolin or sharp knife and drop into the salad dressing. Add the pink grapefruit slices, orange segments and any last juices as well, and toss everything together gently.

Arrange the salad in the centre of each serving plate and add four olives to each one. Nestle three croquettes on top and spoon the sauce over. Scatter any reserved fennel fronds to garnish the croquettes, and serve.

FOR A TWIST...

- Use blood oranges in the salad, when in season.

PRAWN PAD THAI

Bursting with authentic flavours, these pad Thai noodles are a great all-in-one no-cook dinner, and also work well as a lunchbox filler. If you're preparing them in advance, keep the sauce separate from the remaining ingredients, ready to toss together at the last minute, or it will be soaked up by the noodles. Tamarind paste is readily available in supermarkets or Asian stores.

SERVES 4

300g flat rice noodles

175g cooked, peeled prawns

4 spring onions, thinly sliced

1 red chilli, thinly sliced, de-seeded if you prefer less heat (optional)

50g salted peanuts, finely chopped

Large handful of fresh coriander leaves

100g beansprouts

2 limes

SAUCE:

125g tamarind paste

4 tbsp fish sauce

Juice of 4 limes

1 tbsp soy sauce (or tamari for gluten-free)

4 tsp soft light brown sugar

2 garlic cloves, peeled and crushed

Thumb-sized piece of fresh ginger, peeled and finely grated

ESSENTIAL KIT:

Kettle

Fill the kettle with water and put it on to boil.

To prepare the sauce, place the tamarind paste, fish sauce, lime juice, soy sauce and sugar in a large bowl, and whisk until the sugar dissolves. Add the garlic and ginger, and stir everything together, then remove a third of the sauce for serving.

Lay the noodles in a wide dish and pour over enough just-boiled water to cover. Cover and leave to soak for about 10 minutes (or according to the packet's instructions) until tender, stirring halfway through.

Halve the prawns, if they're large, and add them to the sauce. Add half each of the spring onions, chilli (if using), peanuts and coriander. Add all the beansprouts and stir lightly.

When the noodles are tender, drain them thoroughly. Use them warm or refresh in cold water and drain again, if you prefer. Tip them into the bowl with everything else and toss together well.

Pile onto four serving plates and drizzle with the reserved sauce. Scatter the reserved spring onions, chilli, peanuts and coriander over the top. Cut the limes in half and serve on the side with the pad Thai.

FOR A TWIST...

• Replace the prawns with cooked chicken, dried shrimps or tofu.

SMOKED SALMON CRÊPE CAKE
with watercress salad

If you want a great dish for entertaining, this layered smoked salmon and crêpe cake is just the ticket. The finished article looks really impressive, but it is actually pretty easy to achieve. Shop-bought packaged crêpes will work perfectly in this recipe. Serve it whole at the table for guests to slice up themselves. The combination of creamy layers, smoky fish and slightly sweet crêpes makes this a real winner for dinner.

SERVES 6 AS A MAIN (OR 8 AS A STARTER)

200g watercress
Large handful of fresh dill or tarragon leaves
500g full-fat cream cheese
2 tbsp prepared horseradish
Finely grated zest and juice of 2 lemons
8 pancakes or crêpes
500g smoked salmon or smoked trout slices
25g toasted pine nuts
Sea salt and freshly ground black pepper

SALAD:

4 tbsp extra virgin olive oil
Juice of 1 lemon
2 small shallots, peeled and finely chopped
2 tbsp capers
50g watercress

ESSENTIAL KIT:

Kettle
Food processor

Put a kettle on to boil, about a quarter full.

Pick any tough stalks from the watercress and pop the rest in a large bowl with the dill or tarragon leaves. Pour over enough just-boiled water to cover. Cover and set aside for a few minutes until wilted.

Meanwhile, put the cream cheese into a food processor, and add the horseradish, lemon zest and juice.

Drain the wilted greens, refresh in cold water and drain again. Place in the centre of a clean J-cloth and squeeze until they are as dry as possible. Add to the food processor and blitz everything until as fine (and green) as possible. Season to taste.

Lay a pancake or crêpe on a serving platter and spread over about 85g of the cream cheese mixture. Lay about 70g of the smoked fish slices in a single layer on top. Continue to layer the cake in this way, finishing with a layer of the cream cheese on the top. Cover with cling film and chill in the fridge for at least 2 hours or overnight, until firmed up. This can be made up to one day in advance.

When ready to serve, pour the oil and lemon juice into a large serving bowl. Add the shallot, rinse and roughly chop the capers and add those too. Whisk to combine and season to taste. Again, discard any tough stalks from the watercress and toss into the dressing until evenly coated.

Scatter a handful of the dressed watercress along with the pine nuts on top of the crêpe cake. Serve at once with the remaining salad on the side.

MEAT DISHES

PULLED PORK ASIAN LETTUCE CUPS

GF

Although this recipe calls for succulent slow-cooked pulled pork, there's no need to wait around for hours of cooking since these days it's available ready-to-use from supermarkets. If your pulled pork doesn't come with its own sachet of sauce, then use 50g of any sweet or hot chilli sauce. These filled lettuce cups work well for parties, picnics or in a lunchbox.

SERVES 2

1 x 250g packet of pulled pork, finely chopped
2 spring onions, finely chopped
Large handful of fresh coriander leaves
2 large, crisp, iceberg lettuce leaves, or 4 smaller inner leaves, or 8 Little Gem leaves
50g beansprouts
2 handfuls of prawn crackers
25g salted peanuts, roughly chopped
1 red chilli, finely sliced, de-seeded if you prefer less heat (optional)
1 lime

DRESSING:

50g sachet of chilli sauce (from pulled pork packet) or any hot or sweet sauce
Juice of 2 limes
Thumb-sized piece of fresh ginger, peeled and finely grated
1 garlic clove, peeled and crushed
1 tsp fish sauce

To make the dressing, pour the sachet of chilli sauce into a medium bowl and add the lime juice, ginger, garlic and fish sauce. Give everything a good stir together. Spoon a tablespoon of the dressing into each of two tiny serving bowls and set aside.

Add the pulled pork and spring onions to the remaining sauce in the main bowl. Finely chop half the coriander, add to the bowl and toss everything until evenly coated.

Slice the lettuce leaves in half if large and divide them evenly between two serving plates. Spoon the pork mixture into the lettuce cups and place a little pile of beansprouts on top of each one. Pile some prawn crackers beside them.

Sprinkle the peanuts over the top. Scatter with the chilli and remaining coriander leaves. Cut the lime into wedges and arrange two on each plate with a little dish of the reserved sauce for drizzling, and serve.

CHUNKY CHICKEN & DUCK POTS

with winter salad

This is a hearty, meaty mixture set in a vibrant and flavoursome green herb stock. It makes a great lunch or dinner-party course, especially since it is prepared in advance. You can vary the cooked meats and vegetables with any selection you like, for a different outcome each time.

SERVES 6

4 gelatine leaves

Chicken stock cube,
    powder, jelly or liquid
    concentrate (enough
    for 300ml stock)

Very large handful of fresh
    flat-leaf parsley leaves

Very large handful of
    fresh tarragon leaves

600g cooked, skinless
    chicken meat (about
    1 shop-bought cooked
    chicken)

150g cooked, skinless
    duck meat (about
    1 roasted crispy
    half-duck)

1 x 280g jar artichokes

50g shelled pistachios

Sea salt and freshly ground
    black pepper

DRESSING:

200ml Greek yoghurt

50g cornichons, finely
    chopped

1 small garlic clove, peeled
    and finely chopped

Finely grated zest and
    juice of 1 lemon

turn for more →

Half-fill a kettle with water and put it on to boil.

Place the gelatine leaves in a small bowl and pour over enough cold water to cover. Leave to soak for 10 minutes.

In a large jug, make the stock up with 300ml of just-boiled water. Stir in the herbs and leave for a couple of minutes until wilted. Blitz the mixture with a hand blender or in a jug blender until it's as smooth as possible. Pass through a fine sieve and use the back of a spoon to press any remaining juices out of the herbs to give a vibrant green liquid. Squeeze the excess water from the gelatine and pop it into the stock, stirring to dissolve.

Cut or tear the chicken and duck meat into small pieces and place in a large bowl. Drain the artichokes and halve or quarter any whole pieces. Add them to the bowl, along with the pistachios. Season to taste and toss everything together well.

Divide the mixture between the glass jars, pressing everything down well to compact it. Slowly pour in the green stock, allowing it to spread throughout the mixture, until the ingredients are submerged. Leave to cool before securing the lid closed. Chill in the fridge for at least 6 hours or overnight, until set. This can be made up to two days in advance.

To make the salad dressing, spoon the yoghurt into a large bowl. Add the cornichons, garlic and lemon zest and juice. Stir together and season to taste. Cover and chill in the fridge until needed. This can be made up to one day before serving.

Just before serving, prepare the salad. Trim the fennel, reserving any fronds, finely slice the bulb and toss it into the dressing. Add the spring onions and watercress. Give everything a gentle

continued overleaf

1 fennel bulb
Bunch of spring onions,
sliced
75g watercress
25g dried cranberries
Crispbreads or toasted
slices of sourdough
or fruit & nut bread,
to serve (gluten-free if
necessary)

ESSENTIAL KIT:
Kettle
Hand blender or jug
blender
6 x 250ml glass serving
pots or jars (with lids)

stir together until well coated. Arrange a pile of salad on each serving plate or board. Scatter the cranberries and any reserved fennel fronds over the top. Sit a chicken and duck pot beside the salad and serve at once with crispbreads or toast.

FOR A TWIST...

- Use smoked duck for a delicious (albeit more expensive) alternative to plain cooked duck.

- Make into a single large meat 'loaf' or terrine – simply set everything in a 11 x 25cm (8cm deep) (1.5-litre) loaf tin or terrine mould, lined with a double layer of cling film. Cut into slices to serve, dipping a sharp knife in hot water and wiping dry between each cut.

DUCK & SHIITAKE MUSHROOM NOODLE BROTH

If making this in advance, add the cooked noodles to the broth only at the very last minute or they will absorb all the lovely liquid if left to sit in it. This is nice served warm, but is also just as good at room temperature: simply refresh the noodles and pak choi in cold water after 'cooking' and allow the stock to cool before adding the noodles.

SERVES 4 (ABOUT 1.5 LITRES)

Thumb-sized piece of fresh ginger, peeled
1 garlic clove, peeled and crushed
6 dried shiitake mushrooms
1 lemongrass stick
175g thin rice noodles
1 star anise
1 pak choi (at room temperature), roughly chopped
Beef stock cube, powder, jelly or concentrate (enough for 500ml stock)
1 tbsp soy sauce
1 tbsp fish sauce
1 tbsp hoisin sauce
1 tbsp mirin
¼ tsp Chinese five spice
2 spring onions, finely sliced
1 red chilli, finely sliced
Large handful each of fresh coriander and mint leaves
150g cooked, skinless duck meat (about 1 roasted crispy half-duck)
2 tsp sesame oil

ESSENTIAL KIT:

Kettle
Rolling pin or heavy-based pan

Fill a kettle with water and put it on to boil.

Cut the ginger into fine matchsticks and place it in a small bowl with the garlic and shiitake mushrooms. Pour 150ml of just-boiled water over to cover. Sit a clean smaller bowl right into the mixture on top of the ingredients to ensure they stay submerged. Leave to soak for about 10 minutes until tender.

Trim the lemongrass and bash it with a rolling pin or heavy pan to break it open a little, and place it in a wide dish. Add the noodles and star anise. Pour over enough just-boiled water to cover. Cover and leave to soak for 8–10 minutes (or according to the packet instructions), stirring halfway through.

Put the pak choi in a medium bowl. Pour over enough just-boiled water to submerge. Cover and set aside for 3–4 minutes until wilted.

Make up the beef stock with 500ml of just-boiled water and pour into a large bowl. Add the soy, fish and hoisin sauces, mirin and five spice, plus the spring onions and chilli. Roughly chop half of the coriander and mint leaves and add to the bowl too.

Drain the pak choi and pop it into the bowl of stock. Drain the now tender mushrooms over the bowl of stock to catch their soaking liquid. Discard their tough stalks and slice the tops. Add to the stock along with the ginger and garlic. Drain the now softened noodles, discarding the lemongrass and star anise. Tip them into the stock and stir everything well.

Divide the broth between four serving bowls. Cut the duck into thin slices and arrange them overlapping on top. Drizzle a little sesame oil over, scatter with the remaining coriander and mint leaves, and serve.

FOR A TWIST...
• Use smoked duck breast or cooked beef, instead of plain duck.

PIZZA SKEWERS
with tomato dipping sauce

This fun, no-cook alternative to pizza is sure to grab the attention of kids and adults alike. Serve the skewers at a party and watch them disappear in minutes, or pop in a picnic hamper or lunchbox for a novel snack that your family will love.

SERVES 4

Large handful of fresh basil leaves

2 tbsp extra virgin olive oil

1 tbsp toasted pine nuts

Grated zest and juice of ½ lemon

16 mini mozzarella balls

150g focaccia, cut into 2.5cm cubes

16 pitted black, green or mixed olives, stuffed if you prefer

16 cherry tomatoes (mixed colours if available)

16 salami slices and/or other cured meats

Sea salt and freshly ground black pepper

DIPPING SAUCE:

1 garlic clove, peeled and roughly chopped

75g sun-dried tomatoes (from a jar)

Large handful of fresh basil leaves

200ml passata

ESSENTIAL KIT:

Mini-blender

8 metal or wooden skewers

First, marinate the mozzarella. Place the basil leaves in a mini-blender with the oil and pine nuts. Add the lemon zest and juice. Blitz to give a rough paste. Pour into a small bowl and season to taste. Drain the mozzarella balls and stir them through until well coated. Cover and leave to marinate in the fridge for at least 1 hour or overnight.

To make the sauce, pop the garlic and sun-dried tomatoes into a mini-blender, along with half the basil leaves. Blitz until roughly chopped. Add the passata and blitz again until as smooth as possible. Season to taste and place in a small serving bowl. Cover and chill in the fridge until needed. This can be made up to three days in advance or even further ahead if then frozen.

To assemble the skewers, arrange two of each pizza item (marinated mozzarella, focaccia, olives, tomatoes, and meat), in any order, on each skewer. The salami and cured meats look nice either ruffled and pushed onto the skewer or wrapped around the mozzarella balls.

Brush any remaining marinade all over the ingredients, if you like. Arrange the skewers on a large platter or standing up in tall glasses or other suitable vessels. Serve with the tomato dipping sauce and a scattering of the remaining basil leaves to garnish.

FOR A TWIST...

- Mix it up with other favourite pizza toppings such as ham, chicken, prawns, peppers, sun-dried tomatoes, roasted peppers and pimento peppers.

- Add a deliciously smoky flavour to the tomato dipping sauce, with ¼ teaspoon of sweet or hot smoked paprika.

- Make 16 smaller skewers as canapés or for a kid's party, standing each skewer upright with a small glass of sauce.

MEAT 'LOAF'
with olive salsa

This is based on a New Orleans classic, the muffuletta, which is a sandwich traditionally filled with layers of deli meats, salami and cheese. This version is the ultimate meat feast, perfect for a picnic sandwich or a hearty work lunch. Use any cooked cold meats or salami that you like or have left over in the fridge.

SERVES 4

1 round, white bread loaf
   (about 500g, 8cm high
   and 18cm in diameter)
150g each of cooked beef,
   ham and turkey slices
150g pastrami
Sea salt and freshly ground
   black pepper

OLIVE SALSA:

75g pitted black olives
75g pitted green olives
50g sun-dried tomatoes
   (from a jar)
50ml extra virgin olive oil
1 tbsp red wine vinegar
50g cornichons, chopped
1 large garlic clove, peeled
   and roughly chopped
Small handful of fresh basil

SALAD:

4 tbsp extra virgin olive oil
Juice of ½ lemon
1 tsp Dijon mustard
¼ tsp clear honey, (optional)
75g mixed salad leaves
12 cornichons, to serve

ESSENTIAL KIT:

Food processor
Small tray/wooden board
About 4 full cans of food

To make the salsa, place the olives, sun-dried tomatoes, oil and vinegar in a food processor. Add the cornichons, garlic and basil leaves. Give everything a quick blitz so it is roughly chopped. Season to taste (the olives will probably make it salty enough). This can be made up to one week in advance and kept covered in the fridge.

Carefully slice the top off the loaf of bread (about a 2cm-thick piece). Pull the bread out from inside the loaf and the lid, leaving walls about 1cm thick. (The discarded bread can be used for breadcrumbs, the panzanella salad on page 111, the bean and tomato casserole on page 145, or saved for the ducks!) Spread two thirds of the olive salsa all around the inside and the underside of the lid.

Trim any fat or sinew from the meat slices. Arrange half of the beef slices all along the bottom of the loaf, followed by half of the ham, turkey and pastrami. Spread the remaining salsa out evenly on top and then repeat the layers, this time working backwards with the pastrami first, turkey, ham and beef.

Pop the lid back on and wrap it really tightly with cling film. Chill in the fridge for at least 3 hours or overnight, with something heavy on top like a small tray or wooden board with some food cans on top as weights.

When ready to serve, remove the cling film, cut into four wedges and arrange on serving plates. Put the olive oil, lemon juice and mustard for the dressing in a small screw-top jar. Secure the lid and shake vigorously. Season to taste and add the honey for a little sweetness, if you like. Arrange the salad leaves beside the meat loaf, drizzle with the dressing, add a twist of pepper and serve with a few cornichons.

CHICKEN & HAM PICNIC PIE
topped with cheesy potato bites

All the family will enjoy this tasty and nutritious pie. Its no-cook secret is a creamy sauce based on nuts and Cheddar cheese. It transports well, so is ideal for a lunchbox or picnic, as well as for supper. Shaping the potato into balls can take a bit of time, but it makes the pie look fun and inviting, and adds lovely texture to each mouthful. Get the kids to do the ball-rolling to keep them occupied, though don't be surprised if they try to devour them as they go.

SERVES 4

100g blanched almonds
100g cashew nuts
¼ tsp cayenne pepper
50g Cheddar cheese,
    roughly chopped
2 celery sticks, roughly
    chopped
1 small garlic clove, peeled
    and roughly chopped
Vegetable or chicken stock
    cube, powder, jelly or
    liquid concentrate
    (enough for 200ml
    stock)
150g cooked chicken
150g cooked ham
Small handful of fresh
    tarragon leaves, finely
    chopped
75g frozen peas, thawed
Sea salt and freshly ground
    black pepper

POTATO BITES:

400g cooked mashed potato
75g cooked crispy streaky
    bacon (unsmoked)
50g Parmesan cheese,
    finely grated

turn for more →

Put a kettle on to boil, about a quarter full. Line a tray with non-stick baking paper and set aside.

Place the nuts and cayenne in a jug blender, along with the cheese, celery and garlic. Make up the stock with 200ml of just-boiled water and add to the blender. Blitz for 1–2 minutes until as smooth as possible. Pour into a medium bowl.

Tear or chop the chicken and ham into small pieces and add to the sauce along with the chopped tarragon and peas, and stir together well. Season to taste. Spoon the mixture into the baking dish, spreading it evenly, and set aside.

Place the mashed potato in a medium bowl. Clean out the jug blender and then use it to blitz the bacon to fine crumbs. Tip a quarter of them into a wide, shallow dish and the remainder into the mash. Tip half the Parmesan on top of the bacon crumbs and the rest into the mash as well. Stir the mash mixture until well incorporated, and season to taste.

Half-fill a kettle with water and put it on to boil. Shape the mash into 48 small balls, popping them on the prepared tray as you go. Toss the remaining bacon crumbs and Parmesan together until well mixed. Working in batches, carefully roll the potato balls in the mix until evenly coated. Reserve the leftover coating mixture for serving. Arrange the potato balls in a single layer on top of the pie. This can be served straight away or made and assembled up to two days in advance and kept in the fridge. If chilled, allow it to come back to room temperature before serving.

continued overleaf

GREEN BEAN SALAD:

300g fine green beans, trimmed (at room temperature)
25ml extra virgin olive oil
Juice of ½ lemon
1 small garlic clove, peeled and crushed
Small handful of fresh tarragon leaves
50g baby chard (or other red) leaves

ESSENTIAL KIT:
Kettle
Jug blender
1.2-litre baking dish

Place the green beans in a medium bowl. Pour over enough just-boiled water to cover. Cover and set aside for 5 minutes.

To make the salad dressing, pour the olive oil and lemon juice into a large bowl and add the garlic. Finely chop half the tarragon, and add this as well. Whisk together, season to taste and set aside.

Drain and refresh the beans in cold water. When ready to serve, toss them into the dressing along with the baby chard leaves. Pile the salad into a large serving bowl. Sprinkle the remaining coating mixture over the top of the pie and serve.

FOR A TWIST...
• Make individual pies, using 4 x 300ml baking dishes (about 12cm wide), with 12 potato balls to top each one.

CHICKEN BIRYANI
with spicy raita

Biryani is a spiced Indian rice dish, filled with meat and vegetables. It's a meal that wouldn't be the same without the heat of chilli, and here it is provided by the raita, which also brings a lovely coolness to the meal. Enjoy at dinnertime or pop in a lunchbox for food on the go.

SERVES 4

Bunch of spring onions
2 x 250g pouches of cooked basmati rice
1 tsp turmeric powder
1 tsp ground cinnamon
¼ tsp cardamom powder
Juice of ½ lemon
100ml coconut milk
2.5cm piece of fresh ginger
1 garlic clove, peeled
1 green chilli (optional)
Large handful of fresh coriander leaves
50g toasted flaked almonds
300g cooked chicken
Sea salt and freshly ground black pepper

RAITA:

1 tomato, diced
5cm piece of cucumber, diced
200g natural yoghurt
2.5cm piece of fresh ginger, peeled and finely grated
1 green chilli, finely sliced (de-seeded if you prefer)
Handful of fresh coriander leaves, finely chopped
Pinch of chilli powder (optional)

ESSENTIAL KIT:
Kettle

Half-fill a kettle with water and put it on to boil.

Finely slice half the spring onions into rings and set aside. Cut the remainder into very thin matchsticks, submerge in a bowl of iced water, place in the fridge and leave to curl up.

Put the rice in a medium bowl and pour over enough just-boiled water to cover. Cover and leave to soak for 5 minutes.

Place the turmeric, cinnamon and cardamom in a large bowl and pour in the lemon juice. Mix until well blended and then stir in the coconut milk. Peel and finely grate the ginger, and finely chop the garlic and green chilli (if using), discarding the seeds if you prefer. Add all three to the bowl. Roughly chop half the coriander and add, along with half the almonds. Chop or tear the chicken into bite-sized pieces and toss them in along with the sliced spring onions. Finally, drain the rice well and add to the bowl. You can refresh in cold water first, if you prefer not to eat this warm. Toss everything together well and season to taste.

To make the raita, place the tomato and cucumber in a small bowl, and add the yoghurt. Add the grated ginger, half the green chilli and all the chopped coriander, and stir everything together well. Season to taste and spoon into a serving bowl. Scatter the remaining green chilli on top, and garnish with the chilli powder if you like.

Spoon the biryani into the centre of each serving plate. Drain the curled spring onions well and scatter them over the rice, along with the remaining coriander leaves and almonds. Serve with the raita on the side.

FOR A TWIST...
• Use smoked chicken, instead of plain cooked chicken.

SMOKY AUBERGINE & PULLED PORK 'HOT' POTS
with cucumber salad

The addition of harissa makes this dish 'hot' in taste rather than temperature. Add as little or as much harissa as you like, or omit entirely if you prefer. If your baba ganoush is a touch bland, add crushed garlic, ground cumin and/or ground coriander to perk it up. The filling also goes nicely in a wrap or pitta with the cucumber salad or some crisp lettuce.

SERVES 4

200g baba ganoush
25g Greek yoghurt
Juice of ½ lemon
**1 tsp harissa paste (check
for gluten-free)**
½ tsp smoked paprika
2 vine-ripened tomatoes
**Small handful of fresh mint
leaves, finely chopped**
200g pulled pork
**Sea salt and freshly ground
black pepper**

TOPPING:

**125g cooked brown rice
(from a pouch)**
**125g cooked lentils
(drained weight, from
a can or pouch)**
**Large handful of fresh
coriander leaves**

CUCUMBER SALAD:

2 tbsp olive oil
Juice of ½ lemon
¾ cucumber
**Large handful of fresh
mint leaves**

ESSENTIAL KIT:

Kettle
4 x 175ml serving bowls

Half-fill a kettle with water and put it on to boil.

First, prepare the cucumber salad. Pour the oil and lemon juice into a medium bowl and season to taste. Cut the cucumber lengthways into quarters. Remove the seeds from the core and discard, then cut into thin slices and toss into the bowl. Reserve a small handful of mint sprigs for garnishing, finely chop the rest and add to the bowl. Give everything a good toss about. Place in a serving bowl and set aside.

Place the rice for the topping in a medium bowl and pour over enough just-boiled water to submerge. Cover and set aside for 5 minutes.

Spoon the baba ganoush into a large bowl. Add the yoghurt, lemon juice, harissa and smoked paprika, and stir together until well blended. Quarter the tomatoes, discard the seeds and finely chop the flesh. Add to the bowl, along with the chopped mint and pork. Gently stir everything together until well coated. Season to taste. This can be made up to one day in advance and kept covered in the fridge. In this case, return it to room temperature before serving. Divide the filling evenly between serving bowls.

Once tender, drain the rice and rinse in cold water until cool. Tip it back into the bowl and add the lentils. Reserving a small handful of the coriander leaves for garnishing, roughly chop the rest and add to the bowl. Give everything a good toss together and season to taste. Sprinkle the topping over the pork mixture, garnish with coriander and mint sprigs and serve with the cucumber salad.

FOR A TWIST...
- Instead of pork, use chopped ready-cooked turkey, chicken, beef or lamb.

HOT & SOUR CHICKEN NOODLE POTS

This tasty little number elevates the commercial 'pot noodle' to a new and healthier level, ideal for an office lunch or instant supper. While some consider it bad luck to break up noodles, the very convenience of this recipe will have you breaking them in handfuls and feeling fortunate to be tucking into such a fast but satisfying meal. Be sure to start with your vegetables at room temperature, as they won't blanch properly if fridge-cold.

SERVES 1

25g rice vermicelli or thin glass or kelp noodles
25g sugar snap peas or mangetout, finely sliced
25g beansprouts
¼ red pepper, finely sliced
1 spring onion, finely sliced
1 very small carrot, peeled
Small handful of kale or spinach, finely shredded
50g cooked chicken
Small handful of fresh coriander leaves

SAUCE:

1 tsp chilli bean sauce or hot chilli sauce
1 tsp light soy sauce
1 tsp fish sauce (check for gluten-free)
1 small garlic clove, peeled and crushed
¼ thumb-sized piece of fresh ginger, peeled and very finely chopped
Juice of ½ lime

ESSENTIAL KIT:

Kettle
Mandolin or julienne peeler (or sharp knife)
1-litre heatproof glass jar or plastic pot

Break the noodles into pieces if necessary to fit into the base of the serving jar or pot. Add the sugar snap peas or mange tout on top, followed by the beansprouts, red pepper and spring onion in that order. Finely shred the carrot with a mandolin, julienne peeler or long sharp knife, and sprinkle it in, followed by the kale or spinach. Chop or tear the chicken into small pieces and sprinkle it on top, followed by the coriander. This can be made up to two days in advance, and kept covered in the fridge.

To make the sauce, simply mix the chilli bean, soy and fish sauces together in a small bowl until well blended. Add the garlic, ginger and lime juice and mix everything together well. This can also be made up to two days ahead, again kept covered in the fridge.

When ready to serve, half-fill the kettle with water and put it on to boil. Pour the sauce into the jar or pot, followed by 300ml of just-boiled water, to cover everything. Cover and leave for 5 minutes until the noodles are tender and the vegetables softened. Carefully uncover, give it a good stir and enjoy.

FOR A TWIST...

- Add shredded pak choi or cabbage leaves, instead of the kale or spinach.

- Use cooked quinoa or lentils rather than noodles.

FAMILY-STYLE MEXICAN LAYER POT

This hearty fusion of Mexican flavours is a great dish to serve when you're feeding a big crowd. Each of the components can be made up to two days in advance, if the ingredients are fresh, and then kept covered in the fridge ready for assembly. Crushing the coriander tints the sour cream a lovely light green, but you can finely chop the leaves if you find it easier. The black bean houmous also makes a great dip for crispy pittas and crudités, or is tasty spread on a crispbread and topped with avocado.

SERVES 6

Large handful of fresh coriander leaves

300g sour cream

100g Cheddar cheese, roughly grated

200g cooked chicken, in bite-sized pieces

2 x 200g bags tortilla chips gluten-free if necessary

Sea salt and freshly ground black pepper

BLACK BEAN HOUMOUS:

2 x 400g cans black beans

1 garlic clove, peeled and roughly chopped

2 tbsp tahini

1 tbsp extra virgin olive oil

1 tsp ground cumin

Juice of 1 lime

GUACAMOLE:

4 avocados

Juice of 2 limes

½ small red onion, peeled and very finely chopped

turn for more →

As each layer is prepared, cover and store them all in the fridge until ready to assemble.

To prepare the black bean houmous, drain and rinse the beans and pop them in a food processor. Add the garlic, tahini, olive oil, cumin and lime juice. Blend the mixture until smooth, and then season to taste.

For the guacamole, peel and de-stone the avocados and place the flesh of three of them in a food processor along with the lime juice. Blitz until smooth. Place the remaining avocado in a medium bowl and roughly mash with a fork. Add the chopped onion, then spoon the puréed avocado on top and stir everything together. Season to taste.

To make the salsa fresca, quarter the tomatoes, discarding the seeded insides, then finely chop the flesh and place in a large bowl. Add the onion, chilli, coriander and lime juice. Toss everything together and season to taste.

To prepare the coriander cream, grind the coriander leaves to a mush with a pestle and mortar. Alternatively, very finely chop them. Place in a medium bowl, add the sour cream and stir until well blended. Season to taste.

Now for the assembly. Spoon the black bean houmous into the bottom of the serving bowl and spread it evenly with the back of a spoon. Scatter the cheese evenly on top, taking it right to the edges. Next, spoon in and spread out the coriander cream.

continued overleaf

500g vine-ripened tomatoes
½ small red onion, peeled and very finely chopped
1 fresh jalapeño chilli (or 25g jalapeños from a jar), finely chopped and de-seeded if you prefer less heat
Large handful of fresh coriander leaves, roughly chopped
Juice of 1 lime

ESSENTIAL KIT:
Food processor
Pestle and mortar (or sharp knife)
2.8-litre 'trifle'-style serving bowl (about 21cm in diameter)

To spread the guacamole without disturbing the sour cream too much, first dollop it all over and then spread it out gently. Scatter the chicken pieces over in an even layer and finally spoon the salsa fresca on the very top.

Pour the tortilla chips into a large serving bowl and pop it in the centre of the table along with the Mexican layer pot for everyone to help themselves.

FOR A TWIST…
- Serve this in individual glass bowls or even lidded jars or pots to take to work or school.

- Add layers of other ingredients, such as sweetcorn or chopped peppers in your colour of choice.

DESSERTS

EXOTIC FRUIT CUPS

These cups take the humble fruit salad to a whole new level, combining interesting fruits and delicious dressings in attractive cups made from fresh fruit shells. Serve with yoghurt or a crisp sweet biscuit. The coconut halves for the Tropical Treat Cup (recipe overleaf) can be washed out after use and the flesh used for another recipe. If you can't find or don't fancy using a fresh coconut, use dried coconut shavings and coconut water from a carton instead, and serve in a pretty bowl in place of the coconut shell.

dragon fruit cup

SERVES 2
1 dragon fruit
50g raspberries
¼ pomegranate
**Small handful of fresh
    mint sprigs, to decorate**

DRESSING:
Juice of ½ orange
Juice of ½ lemon
1 tsp clear honey
**Small handful of fresh
    mint leaves, finely sliced**

ESSENTIAL KIT:
**30mm melon baller (or
    sharp knife)**

First, make the dressing. Pour the orange and lemon juice into a medium bowl, add the honey and stir until dissolved. Add the mint and stir through.

Cut the dragon fruit in half lengthways. Using a melon baller, scoop the flesh out of each half into balls, and toss into the dressing. Alternatively, use a spoon to scoop out the flesh in as whole a piece as possible, and chop into bite-sized chunks. Use a small, sharp knife to neaten the edges of the fruit halves to give a 5mm border. The trimmings can be tossed into the dressing as well or enjoyed as a chef's treat.

Sit one fruit cup on each serving plate. Gently stir the raspberries through the dressing. Spoon the fruit salad evenly between the fruit cups and drizzle with the remaining dressing.

Remove the seeds from the pomegranate and sprinkle them on top. Serve at once, decorated with mint sprigs.

FOR A TWIST...
* Add a splash of liqueur to the dressing, such as kirsch, Cointreau or crème de cassis (for grown-ups only!).

continued overleaf

tropical treat cup

SERVES 2
1 whole fresh coconut
½ small mango
½ small papaya
4 lychees

DRESSING:
1 passionfruit
Finely grated zest and
   juice of ½ lime
1 tsp clear honey

ESSENTIAL KIT:
Hammer
Screwdriver
Vegetable peeler

To prepare the coconut, first carefully hammer the screwdriver through each of the three 'eyes' at the end of the coconut to create holes. Drain the coconut water out through the holes into a small bowl and reserve. Next, bang the hammer all the way around the centre seam line of the coconut until it splits open in half. Using a vegetable peeler, shave off a small handful of coconut flesh strips and reserve.

To make the dressing, scoop the passionfruit seeds and juice out into a medium bowl. Add the lime zest and juice, honey and 1 tablespoon of the reserved coconut water, and stir everything together well. The remaining coconut water can be saved to use in a juice or smoothie or simply enjoyed as a refreshing drink.

Peel the mango, remove the stone if necessary and slice the flesh into long, thick strips. Scoop the seeds from the papaya half, remove the peel and chop the flesh into bite-sized chunks. Peel the lychees, then run a small, sharp knife around their centres to split the flesh in half and discard the stone. Toss the mango, papaya and lychees through the dressing until evenly coated.

Spoon the fruit evenly between the coconut cups and drizzle with the remaining dressing. Scatter the coconut shavings on top to garnish and serve.

FOR A TWIST...
- Use pineapple instead of any of these fruits.
- Add a splash of liqueur to the dressing, such as rum, Cointreau or Malibu (for grown-ups only!).

CHOCOLATE ORANGE TRUFFLES

(V) (GF)

Much healthier than the usual truffles of chocolate and cream, this blended truffle mix of nuts and Medjool dates will trick everyone into thinking they are being naughty when, in fact, these are sugar-free, gluten-free, vegan and Paleo-friendly. The hint of salt is a delicious contrast to the sweetness of the dates and the bitterness of the chocolate, but you can sprinkle chopped nuts on the top instead, if you prefer. The truffles look great presented in mini paper cases.

MAKES 12

100g dark chocolate (minimum 70% cocoa solids)
50g plain cashew nuts
25g walnuts
25g pecan nuts
Very finely grated zest of 1 large orange
100g pitted Medjool dates
1 tsp vanilla extract
1 tsp fine sea salt (optional)

ESSENTIAL KIT:
Kettle
1 medium and 1 large heatproof bowl
Mini-blender

Half-fill the kettle with water and put it on to boil. Line a tray with non-stick baking paper and set aside.

Sit a medium bowl into a larger one and pour enough just-boiled water in between them to come halfway up the sides of the smaller dish. Very finely grate 25g of chocolate into the top bowl and spread it out evenly. Stir until melted and set aside.

Place all the nuts in a mini-blender and blitz until very finely chopped. Add the orange zest, dates and vanilla extract, and blend until smooth. Add the melted chocolate and blitz again until well combined.

Shape the mixture into 12 even-sized balls (about 20g each), arranging them on the prepared tray as you go. Chill in the fridge for at least 30 minutes until firm.

When the truffles are firm, half-fill the kettle with water again and put it on to boil. Melt the remaining 75g of chocolate as before and leave to cool a little. Pour the melted chocolate into a small, deep bowl. Dip a truffle into the chocolate until completely coated, and allow the excess to drip off before returning to the tray. Using two forks is probably the easiest way of doing this. Quickly sprinkle with a little fine sea salt, if using.

Chill in the fridge for at least 30 minutes, until set firm. These will keep for up to three weeks in the fridge, layered between baking paper in an airtight container.

FOR A TWIST...

• Replace the orange zest with ¼ teaspoon of cardamom powder, or make your own by grinding the seeds from about 5 cardamom pods in a pestle and mortar.

• Give this a boozy kick by adding a splash of Cointreau, Tia Maria or Frangelico to the mix.

MANGO MOUSSE CAKE

This scrumptious cake is made with an eggless mousse, which requires no cooking and is pretty much foolproof, as long as the cream is whipped softly and the mango purée folded in gently, to ensure the finished result is soft and fluffy. If you prefer, you can use 750g of shop-bought mango purée, and then just one fresh mango for the topping. Arranging the mango slices in the way shown is actually much simpler than it appears, and is worth the extra effort to make your cake look amazing! The flan case trimmings can be saved and used for something else – try layering them up with the Balsamic Cherry Fool (page 203).

SERVES 6–8

9 gelatine leaves
200g continental sponge flan case
Sunflower oil, for greasing
4 ripe mangos
500ml double cream
100g icing sugar
Finely grated zest of 1 large orange

TO SERVE:

125g raspberries

ESSENTIAL KIT:

Kettle
20cm round, loose-bottomed cake tin
Food processor or jug blender
Electric or hand whisk

Put the kettle on to boil, about a quarter full.

Soak six of the gelatine leaves in a small bowl, with just enough cold water to cover, for 5 minutes until soft.

Remove the base from the cake tin and place the ring onto the flan case. Press down to stamp out a circle. Save the trimmings for another use (see Introduction). Assemble the cake tin, grease the sides with oil and line them with non-stick baking paper. Sit the sponge disc in the bottom of the tin and set aside.

Drain the water from the now-softened gelatine, squeeze the excess water from it and return to the bowl. Add 2 tablespoons of just-boiled water and stir until dissolved. Leave to cool to room temperature.

Peel and de-stone three of the mangos, weigh out 750g of flesh, and roughly chop. Blitz in a processor or blender until really smooth. Pour 500g of the mango purée into a small bowl and 250g into another and set aside.

Pour the cream into a large bowl and sift the icing sugar in. Whisk until softly whipped.

Add the cooled gelatine mixture into the 500g of mango purée, followed by the orange zest, and stir until well mixed. Then add this mixture to the whipped cream and gently fold together until evenly blended. Pour into the cake tin, spreading the top smooth. Cover and chill in the fridge for about 1 hour until beginning to set.

For the topping, soak the remaining three gelatine leaves in cold water as before, and leave for 5 minutes until soft. Drain as before, squeezing out the excess water, and add 1 tablespoon of

continued overleaf

just-boiled water, stirring until dissolved. Leave to cool to room temperature, then stir the gelatine into the remaining 250g of mango purée until well blended. Pour this over the top of the cake, spreading it evenly.

Peel the remaining mango, cut the cheeks and side bits of flesh from the stone and slice them thinly lengthways. Now for the really pretty bit: twist a mango slice into a circle and sit it (curved side up if applicable) in the mango purée at the centre of the cake. Then curl a couple of slices around it, just a few millimetres apart. Continue to arrange the slices in this way, working outwards until you reach the edge and all of the slices have been used up. This will form a beautiful flower pattern. Cover and chill in the fridge for at least 2 hours or overnight, until set firm.

Remove from the tin and carefully peel off the paper, before sliding the cake onto a stand or platter. When serving, slice the cake using a long, sharp knife, dipped into hot water and wiped dry between cuts. Serve with raspberries on the side.

BALSAMIC CHERRY FOOL

(V) (GF)

Balsamic glaze is a thickened reduction of balsamic vinegar and is readily available in supermarkets. While it might seem an unusual ingredient to use in a dessert, it brings a lovely sharp edge to the sweetness of cherry conserve in this fruit fool. A fool is usually based entirely on cream but this one has the added lightness of Greek or natural yoghurt. This recipe is an easy dessert that can quickly be put together with a few supermarket grabs. Spoon it into screw-top jars for a fun way to eat outdoors.

SERVES 6

500g cherry conserve
2 tbsp balsamic glaze
1 tbsp crème de cassis
 or blackcurrant cordial
 (optional)
500ml Greek or natural
 yoghurt
300ml double cream
4 tbsp clear honey
Seeds from 1 vanilla pod
 or 1 tsp vanilla bean
 paste
6 amaretti or shortbread
 biscuits (choose
 gluten-free biscuits
 if necessary)
18 fresh cherries
 (preferably with stems)

ESSENTIAL KIT:
Electric or hand whisk
1.5-litre trifle bowl or 6 x
 250ml individual glasses
 or bowls

Spoon the cherry conserve into a medium bowl and add the balsamic glaze and crème de cassis or blackcurrant cordial, if using. Stir until well mixed together and set aside.

Place the yoghurt, cream and honey in a large bowl. Add the vanilla seeds or bean paste. Whip to give soft peaks.

Add the cherry mixture to the whipped yoghurty cream and, using a spoon or spatula, ripple together with one or two folds.

Spoon the fool into the trifle bowl or individual glasses or bowls. This can be served straight away or made up to two days in advance and kept covered in the fridge.

When ready to serve, crumble the amaretti or shortbread biscuits over the top(s) to decorate. Arrange the fresh cherries, stems up, on the top to finish and serve.

FOR A TWIST...

- Ripple a jar of apple sauce through before serving.

- Try with other conserves like strawberry, raspberry or blueberry instead of cherry. Top with the matching fresh fruit.

- Get festive and add 1 teaspoon of ground cinnamon or mixed spice to the creamy mixture.

SIN-FREE FRUIT & NUT CHOCOLATE TRIANGLES

(V) (GF)

You can enjoy these fruit and nut chocolate bars without any guilt, as they are packed full of health-boosting ingredients and are so much better for you than their sugary, shop-bought counterparts. Use whatever combination of dried fruits and nuts you fancy. They melt quite easily, due to the coconut oil, so keep them in the fridge until ready to serve. Then just wait for them to melt in the mouth!

MAKES 16

300g peanut, almond or other nut butter

150g coconut oil, softened

100g clear honey

75g shelled pistachios, roughly chopped

75g plain cashew nuts, roughly chopped

75g roasted hazelnuts, roughly chopped

75g dried apricots, roughly chopped

75g raisins

75g goji berries

50g cocoa powder or raw cacao powder

2 tsp vanilla extract

ESSENTIAL KIT:

10 x 32cm fluted, loose-bottomed tart tin (2.5cm in height)

Place the nut butter, coconut oil and honey in a large bowl and stir together until smooth and well blended. Add all the chopped nuts and the apricots, raisins and goji berries. Add the cocoa or cacao powder and vanilla extract to the bowl, and stir everything together well.

Spread the mixture into the tin, smoothing it level with the back of a spoon. Cover and chill in the fridge for at least 8 hours or overnight, until set firm.

Just before serving, bring to room temperature for 10–20 minutes or until soft enough to remove from the tin easily. Then cut into 8 even-sized finger pieces and cut each one diagonally in half to give 16 triangles. This is easiest done using a long sharp knife, dipped in hot water and wiped dry between each cut.

Serve straight away or store between sheets of baking paper in an airtight container in the fridge for up to three weeks.

GREEK YOGHURT PANNACOTTA

with rosewater, honey & pomegranate

This delicate-flavoured dessert uses Greek yoghurt in addition to the usual cream, making for a lighter, more refreshing pannacotta. It also removes the need to reduce the mixture on the hob. Rosewater is readily available in supermarkets or Middle Eastern stores, and gives a distinctive 'Turkish delight' flavour. Omit if you prefer – the flavour of the syrup will still be good. Choose a ripe pomegranate to ensure it has lots of rich ruby red juice; you'll usually find that the darker the skin colour, the riper the pomegranate. Persian candy floss (or pashmak) comes in vanilla (white) or rose (pink) and can be picked up in Asian, Middle Eastern or speciality food stores. Alternatively, use regular shop-bought candy floss.

SERVES 4

2 gelatine leaves
200ml double cream
2 tbsp clear honey
200ml Greek yoghurt
**Seeds from 1 vanilla pod
   or 1 tsp vanilla bean
   paste**
1 pomegranate
**Small handful of Persian
   candy floss (optional)**
**Small handful of fresh
   (unsprayed, organically
   grown) or dried rose
   petals (optional)**

ROSE SYRUP:

2 tbsp clear honey
½ tsp rosewater

ESSENTIAL KIT:

Kettle
**4 x 125ml glasses, jelly
   moulds, darioles or mini
   pudding basins**

Put the kettle on to boil, about a quarter full. Place the gelatine in a small bowl and pour over enough cold water to cover. Leave to soak for 5 minutes until soft.

Meanwhile, pour the cream into a large jug and whisk in the honey until dissolved. Whisk in the Greek yoghurt until smooth. Add the vanilla seeds or bean paste, stir to blend and set aside.

Halve the pomegranate and scoop the seeds and juice out into a small bowl. Drain the juice into a separate small bowl and set both aside (there should be at least 1 tablespoon of juice).

Once soft, drain the gelatine and squeeze excess water from it. Return to the bowl and pour 1 tablespoon of just-boiled water over, stirring until dissolved. Leave to cool to room temperature.

Meanwhile, make the syrup for serving. Mix the honey, rosewater and 1 tablespoon of the pomegranate juice together in a small bowl until well blended, and set aside for serving. Any remaining pomegranate juice is the cook's treat.

Once the gelatine solution has cooled, stir it into the pannacotta mixture until well blended. Divide the mixture evenly between the serving glasses or moulds. Cover and chill in the fridge for at least 3 hours or overnight, until set.

If in moulds, run the outside of the moulds under hot water for a few seconds and then carefully turn them out onto serving plates. If in glasses, set them on a serving plate. Spoon the rosewater syrup over the top and scatter with the pomegranate seeds. Sit a little pile of Persian candy floss on top, if using. Scatter with rose petals, if using, and serve at once.

TOFFEE APPLE TART

(V) (GF)

This no-bake tart is gloriously sticky and yet is completely free from refined sugar. It's also super-easy to make, with just three ingredients each in the base, filling and topping, most of which can be prepared in advance. For a speedier, but naughtier option, you can use a 400g can of caramel as the filling if you prefer.

SERVES 6

BASE:

200g whole almonds
250g pitted Medjool dates
1 tsp ground cinnamon

TOFFEE FILLING:

100g pecan nuts
175g pitted Medjool dates
125ml maple syrup

TO FINISH:

Juice of 1 lemon
2 tbsp maple syrup
2 small red-skinned apples
**200g crème fraîche, to
    serve**
**Ground cinnamon, for
    dusting**

ESSENTIAL KIT:

Food processor
**23cm loose-bottomed,
    fluted tart tin**
Mandolin (or sharp knife)

First, make the base. Place the almonds in a food processor and blitz until fairly fine. Add the dates and cinnamon, and blend again until combined. The mixture should come together easily when squeezed. Place the mixture in the tin and, using dampened hands, press it in evenly all over. Cover and freeze for 30 minutes, or chill in the fridge for at least 1 hour or overnight, until firm. This can be made up to a week in advance.

Meanwhile, make the toffee filling. Place the pecan nuts in the food processor and blitz until very fine. Add the dates and maple syrup and blitz again, scraping down the sides as you go, to give a smooth, thick toffee sauce. Set aside until ready to assemble. This can be made up to a week in advance and kept covered in the fridge.

When ready to serve, prepare the apple topping. Pour the lemon juice into a medium bowl and mix in the maple syrup. Using a mandolin or sharp knife, very thinly slice the apples horizontally across the core. You can de-core the apples beforehand but leaving the cores in gives a cute star pattern in the slices – just pick the pips out as you go. Gently toss the slices through the lemon and maple syrup mixture until well coated.

To assemble, spoon the toffee filling into the base and spread evenly with the back of a spoon. Carefully remove the tart from the tin, sliding it onto a serving plate. Drain the apple slices well from the syrup and arrange them decoratively on top of the tart. Dollop the crème fraîche into a small bowl, dust with a little ground cinnamon, and serve on the side.

FOR A TWIST...

- Make individual tarts – use four 10cm or six 8cm loose-bottomed, fluted tart tins instead of one large one.

- Turn this tart into a crumble by reversing the build. Chop, rather than slice, the apples and toss it in the toffee sauce. Place in a baking dish and crumble the base on the top.

PINEAPPLE, COCONUT & GINGER GRANITA

(V) (GF)

Granita is an Italian frozen dessert, a bit like a sorbet but with a shaved ice effect. Like sorbet, it makes for a very refreshing and cooling treat. You can't really go wrong making this and it is an excellent, stress-free dinner party treat, as it can be prepared well in advance. The kids will love it too, especially if you get them involved with scraping the icy flakes.

SERVES 8–10

1 pineapple
250ml coconut water
Pared zest and juice
    of 1 lime
2 stem ginger balls (from
    a jar, with syrup),
    roughly chopped

TO SERVE:

Small handful of fresh mint
    leaves (optional)
Large handful of dried
    coconut shavings
    (optional)

ESSENTIAL KIT:

Food processor or jug
    blender
Wide plastic tub, enamel
    tin or baking dish of at
    least 800ml volume

Peel the pineapple, quarter it lengthways and remove the core from each piece. Roughly chop the flesh (you want about 500g). Place in a processor or blender and add the coconut water.

Reserve the lime zest, and add the juice into the blender. Add the chopped stem ginger, reserving the syrup in the jar. Blitz until smooth.

Pour into a plastic tub, enamel tin or baking dish, cover and freeze for 2 hours. Rake the mixture all over with a fork and return to the freezer for another hour. Repeat every hour or two until completely frozen, at least 8 hours or overnight. This will keep for a few months in the freezer.

When ready to serve, rake it once again with a fork and scoop it into serving glasses or bowls. Drizzle with a little of the reserved ginger syrup and scatter the lime zest on top. Decorate with mint leaves and coconut shavings if you like. Serve straight away.

FOR A TWIST...

- Use 2 ripe mangos instead of the pineapple for an alternative tropical treat.

SALTED CARAMEL POPCORN FUDGE

(V) (GF)

This is a cheat's version of fudge, made without the usual melting and stirring of sugar that traditional fudge recipes call for. The combination of salted caramel and popcorn, on top of the soft fudge, is irresistible. Serve at parties or keep in the fridge as a naughty nibble.

MAKES 36 PIECES
Sunflower oil, for greasing
200g salted caramel
400g condensed milk
Seeds from 1 vanilla pod
    or 1 tsp vanilla bean
    paste
400g white chocolate
15g salted popcorn

ESSENTIAL KIT:
Kettle
1 small, 2 medium and
    1 large heatproof bowl
1 medium and 1 large
    baking dish
Food processor
17.5cm square cake tin or
    baking dish

Fill the kettle with water and put it on to boil. Grease the cake tin or dish with oil and line with non-stick baking paper, leaving 5cm excess hanging over the edges to help with lifting out later.

Sit a small heatproof bowl inside a medium one. Carefully pour enough just-boiled water in between the bowls to come halfway up the sides of the small bowl. Spoon the salted caramel into the top bowl. Set aside to melt, stirring occasionally.

Sit a medium heatproof bowl inside a large one. Carefully pour enough just-boiled water in between the bowls to come halfway up the sides of the inner bowl. Pour the condensed milk into the inner bowl and add the vanilla seeds or bean paste. Stir to blend and then set aside to warm through, stirring occasionally.

Break the chocolate into the food processor and blitz until finely chopped. Sit a medium baking dish inside a slightly bigger one and carefully pour enough just-boiled water in between to come halfway up the sides of the smaller dish. Sprinkle the chocolate all over the inside of the top dish and stir until melted.

Stir the melted chocolate into the warmed condensed milk and pour into the prepared tin, spreading evenly. Working quickly before the mixture sets, drizzle the melted salted caramel all over the top and using a spoon handle, swirl it into the chocolate mixture to ripple it through. Sprinkle the popcorn in an even layer on top, pressing it down gently to stick. Chill in the fridge for at least 3–4 hours, until set firm (the salted caramel will still be sticky).

Lift the slab out of the tin and peel off the paper. Using a long, sharp knife, dipped in boiling water and wiped dry between each cut, slice into 36 pieces. These will keep for up to one week, covered and layered between baking paper, in the fridge.

FOR A TWIST...
• Swap the popcorn for 100g of roughly chopped, salted peanuts.

STRIPED SMOOTHIE JELLY

GF

Homemade jelly is a great way of getting fruit into children without them even realising and this one is sure to impress with its vibrant colour and distinctive 'racing' stripe. Use any flavour of red smoothie you like – there are lots of red options to choose from, such as berries, pomegranate, cherry and even beetroot. Many smoothies now include extras like vitamins, flaxseeds or acai, giving them added health-boosting properties.

SERVES 10–12

18 gelatine leaves
2 litres red smoothie
300ml natural or Greek
yoghurt (plus extra for
serving, optional)

ESSENTIAL KIT:

Kettle
2.4-litre jelly mould or non-
metallic bundt tin
(about 9 x 21.5cm)

Put the kettle on to boil, about a quarter full.

Place eight of the gelatine leaves in a small bowl and pour over just enough cold water to cover. Leave to soak for 5 minutes until soft.

Once softened, drain the gelatine well and squeeze the excess water from it. Return it to the bowl and pour over 5 tablespoons of just-boiled water, stirring until dissolved. Leave for a few minutes to cool to room temperature. Pour 1 litre of the smoothie into a large jug and stir in the cooled gelatine liquid. Pour into the jelly mould or bundt tin. Cover, pop into the fridge, making sure it is on a level shelf, and chill for at least 3 hours until beginning to set.

For the next layer, place six leaves of gelatine in a bowl of cold water as before, and leave to soak for 5 minutes until softened. Drain as before, squeezing out the excess water, and then add 4 tablespoons of just-boiled water, stirring until dissolved. Leave to cool to room temperature.

While this is cooling, stir the yoghurt and 500ml of the smoothie together in a large jug until well blended. Stir in the cooled gelatine liquid and carefully pour the mixture in on top of the set jelly. Cover and chill, again making sure it is level, for at least 3 hours until beginning to set.

For the final layer, soak the remaining four gelatine leaves in cold water as before until soft. Drain as before, then add 3 tablespoons of just-boiled water and stir until dissolved. Once cooled, stir this into the remaining 500ml of smoothie in a jug. As this layer should come to the top of the mould, it is best to pour it into the mould as it sits in the fridge to avoid spilling.

continued opposite

Carefully pour it on top of the jelly and leave to set in the fridge for a final 4–6 hours or overnight, until set firm.

To turn out, run the outside of the mould under hot water for a few seconds. Then place the serving plate or stand upside down on top of the mould and carefully turn the whole thing over – a little shake should release the jelly. Remove the mould to reveal the jelly in all its stripy glory. Serve with dollops of yoghurt if you like.

FOR A TWIST...
- Use a green super smoothie instead of the red one. The addition of 4 teaspoons of matcha tea powder not only enhances the green colour but boosts the flavour and health benefits as well. Mix the matcha powder in a small amount of smoothie first, to prevent lumps, then combine it all together.

MINTY CHOCO-MOLE MOUSSE POTS

(V) (GF)

These pots combine the silky smoothness of a blended avocado with the flavour of chocolate. If the idea of chocolate and avocado in the same mouthful sounds unconventional, trust me – they are a food marriage made in heaven. Piping the mixture into the glasses gives a tidy finish and helps avoid air gaps, but the mixture can be spooned in if you prefer. The biscuit on top offers a contrasting crunch to the smooth mousse. Healthier versions of chocolate biscuits are now widely available, if you prefer to keep this dessert on the virtuous side.

SERVES 4

25g chocolate biscuits (choose gluten-free if necessary)
2 ripe avocados
75ml maple syrup
50g cocoa or raw cacao powder
½ tsp vanilla extract
½ tsp peppermint extract
4 mint sprigs with 5cm stalks

ESSENTIAL KIT:

Mini-blender
Disposable piping bag (or two small spoons)
4 x 100ml serving glasses

Place the biscuits in a mini-blender and blitz to give a rough crumb. Tip them into a small bowl and set aside. Wipe the blender bowl and blade of biscuit crumbs.

Halve the avocados, discard their stones and scoop the flesh into the blender. Add the maple syrup, cocoa or raw cacao powder, vanilla extract and peppermint extract, and blitz to give a thick, silky smooth mousse. Cut the tip off the piping bag to give a 2cm opening. Scoop the mixture into the bag and then pipe it evenly between the serving glasses. Alternatively, use two small spoons to scoop and scrape the mixture into the glasses.

This can be eaten straight away or it can be made up to two days in advance and kept covered in the fridge. When ready to serve, sprinkle the biscuit crumbs evenly over the top of each one. Stick a mint stalk into the centre of each one, so it sits upright as if growing, and serve.

FOR A TWIST...

- Instead of the peppermint extract, add to the blender either the finely grated zest of 1 large orange, a 2.5 cm piece of fresh ginger that has been peeled and finely grated, or ½ tsp instant espresso powder. Or stir 1 red chilli, de-seeded and finely chopped, through the mixture after it's blended.

A

almonds
  ginger power balls 38
  ricotta & almond courgette
    ravioli 134
  toffee apple tart 208
apples
  blackberry & apple jam 21
  fresh apple 'doughnuts' 32
  toffee apple tart 208
  Waldorf salad with ham 102
apricots
  dolma rolls with fennel dip 61
  sin-free fruit & nut chocolate
    triangles 204
artichokes
  chicken & duck pots 176–8
  walnut-stuffed chicory with
    artichoke & feta purée 65
Asian miso soup 80
asparagus
  Italian slice with courgette
    lattice top 143–4
  smoked mackerel pâté pots with
    lemony asparagus salad 165
  spring veg risotto 132
aubergine: smoky aubergine
  & pulled pork 'hot' pots 188
avocados
  avocado & cucumber soup 78
  BLT salad with avocado aioli 39
  cauliflower-rice buddha bowl 98
  hot-smoked salmon burger
    with avocado 'chips' 154
  Mexican beef tartare with spicy
    avocado sauce 66
  Mexican layer pot 191–2
  Mexican tostadas 45
  minty choco-mole mousse 216
  spring veg risotto 132
  sushi cones with pickled
    radishes & miso mayo 151–2

B

bacon
  Bloody Mary beans 47
  BLT salad with avocado aioli 39
  blue cheese & bacon truffle
    pops 59
  Brussels sprout salad with bacon,
    pecans & cranberries 100
  chicken & ham picnic pie 184–6
bananas
  banana, oat & pecan mini
    muffins 23
  chia pudding pops with coconut,
    raspberry & banana 36

beans
  bean & tomato 'casserole' 145
  beetroot & bean sliders 137–8
  black bean burger 116–17
  Bloody Mary beans 47
  green bean salad 186
  Mexican layer pot 191–2
  Mexican tostadas 45
  Tuscan white bean soup 87
beef
  beef, blueberry & feta salad 107
  meat 'loaf' with olive salsa 183
  Mexican beef tartare 66
  Vietnamese beef pho 82
beetroot 12
  beetroot, coconut & lemongrass
    soup 92
  beetroot & bean sliders 137–8
  beetroot pâté pots 70
  cauliflower-rice buddha bowl 98
bircher muesli 35
black pudding: Scotch eggs 42–4
blackberries
  blackberry & apple jam 21
  lemon & walnut goats' cheese
    blinis with blackberries 55
Bloody Mary beans 47
BLT salad with avocado aioli 39
blue cheese & bacon truffle pops 59
blueberries: beef, blueberry &
  feta salad 107
bouillabaisse with cheat's rouille
  85–6
bread
  bean & tomato 'casserole' 145
  lentil, peach & halloumi
    panzanella 111
  meat 'loaf' with olive salsa 183
  pizza skewers 180
breakfast toppings 21–2
broccoli: spring veg risotto 132
Brussels sprout salad with bacon,
  pecans & cranberries 100
bulghur wheat: mixed bean &
  tomato 'casserole' 145
butternut squash 'spaghetti' with
  clams & sun-dried tomato 153
butters
  spiced orange hazelnut butter 22
  whipped espresso butter 21

C

cabbage
  falafel wraps with pickled red
    cabbage 128–30
  five-spiced duck noodle salad 108
carrots
  'carrot-cake' overnight oats 35

quinoa & spinach no-meat balls
  with carrot 'spaghetti' 114
cashew nuts
  cashew & fig breakfast bars 24
  chicken & ham pie 184–6
  chocolate orange truffles 199
  creamy corn & chicken soup 95
  sin-free fruit & nut chocolate
    triangles 204
cauliflower-rice buddha bowl 98
celeriac & hazelnut slaw with
  smoked mackerel 104
celery
  Bloody Mary beans 47
  creamy corn & chicken soup 95
  Waldorf salad with ham 102
cheese
  beef, blueberry & feta salad 107
  beetroot pâté pots 70
  blue cheese & bacon truffle
    pops 59
  cheesy chilli poppers 75
  chestnut, blue cheese &
    watercress 'pizzas' 123
  chicken & ham picnic pie 184–6
  courgette lasagne 139–40
  courgette 'pappardelle' 127
  dolma rolls with fennel dip 61
  herby soft cheese tart 118–20
  Italian slice with a courgette
    lattice top 143–4
  lemon & walnut goats' cheese
    blinis with blackberries 55
  lentil, peach & halloumi
    panzanella 111
  Mexican layer pot 191–2
  Mexican tostadas 45
  pizza skewers 180
  ricotta & almond courgette
    ravioli 134
  stuffed marinated courgettes
    with oozing cheese 131
  three-cheese cocktail quiches 72
  walnut-stuffed chicory with
    artichoke & feta purée 65
  watermelon pizza with fig, feta
    & raspberry dressing 124
cherries: balsamic cherry fool 203
chestnuts: chestnut, blue cheese
  & watercress 'pizzas' 123
chia seeds
  blackberry & apple jam 21
  chia pudding pops with coconut,
    raspberry & banana 36
  ginger power balls 38
chicken
  chicken & duck pots 176–8
  chicken & ham picnic pie 184–6

chicken biryani 187
chicken chow mein noodles 110
chicken 'koftas' with peanut
    dipping sauce 56
creamy corn & chicken soup 95
easy-peasy paella 156
hot & sour noodle pots 190
Mexican layer pot 191–2
chickpeas
    beef, blueberry & feta salad 107
    cauliflower-rice buddha bowl 98
    falafel wraps 128–30
    speckled Scotch eggs 42–4
chillies
    cheesy chilli poppers 75
    Mexican tostadas 45
    salsa fresca 191–2
    Thai red curry mussel broth 88
    Vietnamese beef pho 82
chocolate
    chocolate orange truffles 199
    minty choco-mole mousse 216
    salted caramel popcorn fudge 212
    sin-free fruit & nut chocolate
        triangles 204
chorizo
    easy-peasy paella 156
    Mexican tostadas 45
cinnamon mascarpone 22
clams: butternut squash 'spaghetti'
    with clams 153
coconut
    'carrot-cake' overnight oats 35
    fruit sushi with coconut &
        passion fruit dip 29–30
    pineapple, coconut
        & ginger granita 211
    tropical treat fruit cup 198
coconut milk
    beetroot, coconut & lemongrass
        soup 92
    chia pudding pops with coconut,
        raspberry & banana 36
    chicken biryani 187
    Thai red curry mussel broth 88
coconut oil
    poppy seed 'pancakes' 26
    sin-free fruit & nut chocolate
        triangles 204
coffee: whipped espresso butter 21
courgettes
    courgette 'pappardelle' 127
    Italian slice with courgette
        lattice top 143–4
    no-cook lasagne 139–40
    ricotta & almond courgette
        ravioli 134
    stuffed marinated courgettes 131

couscous: stuffed marinated
    courgettes 131
crab
    crunchy crab & corn cakes 60
    prawn, smoked salmon & crab
        terrine 162–4
cranberries: Brussels sprout
    salad with maple dressing 100
cream cheese
    beetroot pâté pots 70
    cheesy chilli poppers 75
    courgette lasagne 139–40
    fresh apple 'doughnuts' 32
    smoked mackerel pâté pots 165
    smoked salmon crêpe cake 170
    smoked salmon mousse 69
cucumber
    avocado & cucumber soup 78
    gazpacho 94
    gravadlax salmon with hot-and-
        sour cucumber 159–60
    raita 187
    salad 188
    'seared' tuna steak with quinoa
        & pickled cucumber 148
    smoked salmon mousse in
        cucumber cups 69
    smoky aubergine & pork 'hot'
        pots with cucumber salad 188
    sushi cones with pickled
        radishes & miso mayo 151–2

D

dates
    cashew & fig breakfast bars 24
    chocolate orange truffles 199
    ginger power balls 38
    toffee apple tart 208
dolma rolls with fennel dip 61
dragon fruit cup 196
duck 12–13
    chicken & duck pots 176–8
    duck & shiitake noodle broth 179
    five-spiced duck noodles 108

E

eggs 13
    Mexican tostadas 45
    Parma ham & kale Caesar 103
    smoked mackerel kedgeree 40
    speckled Scotch eggs with
        black pudding 42–4

F

falafel wraps 128–30
fennel
    bouillabaisse with cheat's
        rouille 85–6

chicken & duck pots 176–8
Mediterranean tuna croquettes
    & fennel citrus salad 166–8
pickled 85–6
feta
    beef, blueberry & feta salad 107
    beetroot pâté pots 70
    dolma rolls with fennel dip 61
    walnut-stuffed chicory with
        artichoke & feta purée 65
    watermelon pizza with fig, feta
        & raspberry dressing 124
figs
    cashew & fig breakfast bars 24
    watermelon pizza with fig, feta
        & raspberry dressing 124
fish
    celeriac & hazelnut slaw with
        smoked mackerel 104
    'seared' tuna steak 148
    smoked mackerel kedgeree 40
    smoked mackerel pâté pots 165
    sushi cones 151–2
    tuna croquettes 166–8
    tuna tartare 161
flaxseeds
    ginger power balls 38
    herby soft cheese tart with
        nutty pastry 118–20
    lentil & kale pot pies 121–2
    peach melba smoothie bowl 31
    poppy seed 'pancakes' 26
fruit
    exotic fruit cups 196–8
    fresh apple 'doughnuts' 32
    fruit sushi 29–30
    see also specific fruit
fudge: salted caramel popcorn 212

G

gazpacho 94
ginger power balls 38
goats' cheese
    Italian slice with courgette
        lattice top 143–4
    lemon & walnut goats' cheese
        blinis with blackberries 55
goji berries
    cauliflower-rice buddha bowl 98
    ginger power balls 38
granita: pineapple, coconut &
    ginger 211
grapefruit
    fennel citrus salad 166–8
    pink grapefruit-cured scallops 74
grapes
    blue cheese & bacon truffle
        pops 59

herby soft cheese tart with
    nutty pastry & grapes 118–20
Waldorf salad with ham 102
gravadlax salmon 159–60

H

halloumi: lentil, peach &
    halloumi panzanella 111
ham
    cheesy chilli poppers 75
    chicken & ham picnic pie 184–6
    meat 'loaf' with olive salsa 183
    Parma ham & kale Caesar
        salad 103
    Tuscan white bean soup 87
    Waldorf salad with ham 102
hazelnuts
    beef, blueberry & feta salad 107
    beetroot pâté pots 70
    celeriac & hazelnut slaw 104
    sin-free fruit & nut chocolate
        triangles 204
    spiced orange hazelnut butter 22
    watermelon pizza with fig, feta
        & raspberry dressing 124
hollandaise sauce 42–4

I

Italian slice with courgette lattice
    top 143–4

J

jelly, striped smoothie 214–5

K

kale
    lentil & kale pot pies 121–2
    Parma ham & kale Caesar
        salad 103

L

lemon & walnut goats' cheese
    blinis with blackberries 55
lemon curd: poppy seed 'pancakes'
    with lemon ricotta yoghurt 26
lentils
    lentil, peach & halloumi
        panzanella 111
    lentil & kale pot pies 121–2
    smoky aubergine & pulled pork
        'hot' pots 188
lettuce
    BLT salad & avocado aioli 39
    pulled pork lettuce cups 174
    see also salads
lychees: tropical treat fruit cup 198

M

mackerel
    celeriac & hazelnut slaw with
        smoked mackerel 104
    smoked mackerel kedgeree 40
    smoked mackerel pâté pots 165
mango
    fruit sushi 29–30
    mango mousse cake 200–2
    tropical treat fruit cup 198
maple syrup
    Brussels salad with bacon &
        maple dressing 100
    fresh apple 'doughnuts' 32
    minty choco-mole mousse 216
    poppy seed 'pancakes' 26
    toffee apple tart 208
mascarpone
    cinnamon mascarpone 22
    three-cheese cocktail quiches 72
meat 'loaf' with olive salsa 183
Mediterranean tuna croquettes
    with fennel citrus salad 166–8
melon: chilled melon soup with
    pickled prawns 91
Mexican beef tartare with spicy
    avocado sauce 66
Mexican layer pot 191–2
Mexican tostadas with chorizo,
    avocado & black beans 45
milk: 'carrot-cake' overnight oats 35
minestrone verde 81
minty choco-mole mousse pots 216
miso
    dip 52
    mayonnaise 151–2
    soup 80
muffins: banana, oat & pecan 23
mushrooms
    chestnut, blue cheese &
        watercress 'pizzas' 123
    duck & shiitake noodle broth 179
mussels: Thai red curry mussel
    broth 88

N

noodles
    chicken chow mein noodles 110
    duck & shiitake noodle broth 179
    five-spiced duck noodles 108
    gravadlax salmon 159–60
    hot & sour chicken noodle pots
        190
    prawn pad Thai 169
    Vietnamese beef pho 82
    Vietnamese pulled pork
        summer rolls 62–4

nuts
    banana, oat & pecan mini
        muffins 23
    beef, blueberry & feta salad 107
    beetroot pâté pots 70
    Brussels sprout salad with
        pecans & maple dressing 100
    cashew & fig breakfast bars 24
    celeriac & hazelnut slaw 104
    chicken & duck pots 176–8
    chicken & ham picnic pie 184–6
    chicken 'koftas' with peanut
        dipping sauce 56
    chocolate orange truffles 199
    courgette lasagne 139–40
    creamy corn & chicken soup 95
    fresh apple 'doughnuts' 32
    ginger power balls 38
    herby soft cheese tart with
        nutty pastry 118–20
    lemon & walnut goats' cheese
        blinis with blackberries 55
    lentil, peach & halloumi
        panzanella with walnut
        dressing 111
    lentil & kale pot pies 121–2
    prawn pad Thai 169
    ricotta & almond courgette
        ravioli 134
    sin-free fruit & nut chocolate
        triangles 204
    spiced orange hazelnut butter 22
    toffee apple tart 208
    Waldorf salad with ham 102
    walnut-stuffed chicory cups with
        artichoke & feta purée 65
    watermelon pizza with fig, feta &
        raspberry dressing 124

O

oats
    banana, oat & pecan mini
        muffins 23
    'carrot-cake' overnight oats 35
    cashew & fig breakfast bars 24
    falafel wraps 128–30
    ginger power balls 38
olives
    Italian slice with a courgette
        lattice top 143–4
    meat 'loaf' with olive salsa 183
    Mediterranean tuna croquettes
        with fennel citrus salad 166–8
    pizza skewers 180
    walnut-stuffed chicory cups with
        artichoke & feta purée 65
    watermelon pizza with fig, feta &
        raspberry dressing 124

onions 13
    black bean burger with pickled
        red onion 116–17
    BLT salad with avocado aioli 39
    salsa fresca 191–2
oranges
    chocolate orange truffles 199
    fennel citrus salad 166–8
    spiced orange hazelnut butter 22

P

paella, easy-peasy 156
pak choi
    duck & shiitake noodle broth 179
    five-spiced duck noodle salad
        with pak choi slaw 108
pancakes: smoked salmon crêpe
    cake with watercress salad 170
pannacotta: with rosewater, honey
    & pomegranate 207
papaya
    tropical treat fruit cup 198
    tuna tartare with wasabi
        papaya slaw 161
Parma ham & kale Caesar salad 103
passion fruit
    fruit sushi with coconut &
        passion fruit dip 29–30
    tropical treat fruit cup 198
pasta: minestrone verde 81
peaches
    lentil, peach & halloumi
        panzanella 111
    peach melba smoothie bowl 31
peanut butter
    chicken 'koftas' with peanut
        dipping sauce 56
    fresh apple 'doughnuts' 32
    sin-free fruit & nut chocolate
        triangles 204
peanuts: prawn pad Thai 169
peas
    courgette 'pappardelle' with
        minted pea pesto 127
    easy-peasy paella 156
pecans
    banana, oat & pecan mini
        muffins 23
    Brussels sprout salad with bacon,
        pecans & maple dressing 100
    chocolate orange truffles 199
    toffee apple tart 208
peppers 12
    bean & tomato 'casserole' 145
    cheesy chilli poppers 75
    chicken chow mein noodles 110
    easy-peasy paella 156
    gazpacho 94

    Italian slice with a courgette
        lattice top 143–4
pine nuts
    courgette 'pappardelle' with
        minted pea pesto 127
    herby soft cheese tart with nutty
        pastry 118–20
    lentil & kale pot pies 121–2
pineapple
    hot-smoked salmon burger with
        pineapple salsa 154
    pineapple, coconut & ginger
        granita 211
pink grapefruit-cured scallops 74
pistachios: sin-free fruit & nut
    chocolate triangles 204
pizza skewers 180
pizzas
    chestnut, blue cheese &
        watercress 'pizzas' with
        mushroom bases 123
    watermelon pizza with fig, feta &
        raspberry dressing 124
pomegranate
    dragon fruit cup 196
    Greek yoghurt pannacotta with
        rosewater & pomegranate 207
popcorn: salted caramel popcorn
    fudge 212
poppy seed 'pancakes' with lemon
    ricotta yoghurt 26
pork
    pulled pork lettuce cups 174
    smoky aubergine & pulled pork
        'hot' pots 188
    Vietnamese summer rolls 62–4
potatoes
    chicken & ham picnic pie 184–6
    crunchy crab & corn cakes 60
    tuna croquettes 166–8
prawns
    chilled melon soup with pickled
        prawns 91
    prawn, smoked salmon & crab
        terrine 162–4
    prawn pad Thai 169
    sesame prawn toasts 50
    sushi cones 151–2

Q

quiches: three-cheese cocktail 72
quinoa
    quinoa & spinach no-meat balls
        with carrot 'spaghetti' 114
    'seared' tuna steak with quinoa
        salad 148
    vegetable quinoa sushi rolls with
        miso dip 52–4

R

radishes: sushi cones with pickled
    radishes & miso mayo 151–2
raspberries
    chia pudding pops with coconut,
        raspberry & banana 36
    dragon fruit cup 196
    peach melba smoothie bowl 31
    watermelon pizza with fig, feta
        & raspberry dressing 124
ricotta
    poppy seed 'pancakes' with
        lemon ricotta yoghurt 26
    ricotta & almond courgette
        ravioli 134
    three-cheese cocktail quiches 72

S

salads
    beef, blueberry & feta 107
    BLT salad with avocado aioli 39
    Brussels sprout with bacon &
        maple dressing 100
    cauliflower-rice buddha bowl
        with zingy carrot dressing 98
    chicken chow mein noodles 110
    cucumber 188
    dressed sweetcorn 116–17
    fennel citrus 166–8
    five-spiced duck noodles with
        pak choi slaw 108
    green bean 186
    lemony asparagus 165
    lentil, peach & halloumi
        panzanella 111
    Parma ham & kale Caesar 103
    tomato 121–2
    Waldorf with smoked ham &
        buttermilk dressing 102
    watercress 170
    winter 176–8
salmon
    gravadlax salmon 159–60
    hot-smoked salmon burger 154
    prawn, smoked salmon & crab
        terrine 162–4
    smoked salmon crêpe cake 170
    smoked salmon mousse 69
    sushi cones with pickled radishes
        & miso mayonnaise 151–2
salted caramel popcorn fudge 212
sauces & dips
    avocado 66
    cheat's rouille 85–6
    chilli lime 50
    chimichurri 75
    dill cream 166–8

fennel & feta dip 61
guacamole 191–2
hollandaise 42–4
miso dip 52
miso mayonnaise 151–2
New Orleans dipping 60
olive salsa 183
parsley pesto 81
pea pesto 127
peanut dipping sauce 56
pineapple salsa 154
raita 187
salsa fresca 191–2
spinach pesto 128–30
sun-dried tomato 153
tomato 139–40
tomato dipping 180
tomato salsa 45, 134
Vietnamese dipping 62–4
watercress pesto 123
scallops: pink grapefruit-cured 74
Scotch eggs with black pudding and
    hollandaise 42–4
seafood 13
    bouillabaisse 85–6
    butternut squash 'spaghetti' with
        clams 153
    crunchy crab & corn cakes 60
    easy-peasy paella 156
    pink grapefruit scallops 74
    prawn, smoked salmon & crab
        terrine 162–4
    sushi cones with pickled radishes
        & miso mayonnaise 151–2
    Thai red curry mussel broth 88
    see also prawns
sesame prawn toasts 50
smoothie jelly, striped 214–5
soups
    avocado & cucumber 78
    beetroot, coconut & lemongrass 92
    bouillabaisse 85–6
    chilled melon with pickled
        prawns 91
    creamy corn & chicken 95
    duck & shiitake noodle broth 179
    gazpacho 94
    minestrone verde 81
    simple Asian miso 80
    Tuscan white bean 87
    Vietnamese beef pho 82
spinach 12
    falafel wraps with spinach pesto
        & pickled red cabbage 128–30
    quinoa & spinach no-meat balls
        with carrot 'spaghetti' 114
    smoked mackerel kedgeree 40
    spring veg risotto 132

strawberries: fruit sushi with
    coconut & passion fruit dip 29–30
summer rolls: Vietnamese pulled
    pork 62–4
sushi cones with pickled radishes &
    miso mayo 151–2
sweetcorn
    black bean burger with chipotle
        cream & dressed sweetcorn
        salad 116–17
    creamy corn & chicken soup 95
    crunchy crab & corn cakes 60

T

tarts
    herby soft cheese with nutty
        pastry & grapes 118–20
    toffee apple 208
Thai red curry mussel broth 88
toffee apple tart 208
tofu: simple Asian miso soup 80
tomatoes
    bean & tomato 'casserole' 145
    Bloody Mary beans 47
    BLT salad with avocado aioli 39
    bouillabaisse with cheat's rouille
        85–6
    butternut squash 'spaghetti' with
        clams & sun-dried tomato 153
    courgette lasagne 139–40
    falafel wraps 128–30
    gazpacho 94
    lentil & kale pot pies with fresh
        tomato salad 121–2
    Mexican tostadas 45
    pizza skewers with tomato
        dipping sauce 180
    raita 187
    ricotta & almond courgette
        ravioli with crushed tomato
        sauce 134
    salsa fresca 191–192
    Scotch eggs with black pudding
        and hollandaise 42–4
    three-cheese cocktail quiches 72
    walnut-stuffed chicory cups with
        artichoke & feta purée 65
    watermelon pizza with fig, feta &
        raspberry dressing 124
tropical treat fruit cup 198
tuna
    'seared' tuna steak 148
    tuna croquettes 166–8
    tuna tartare 161
turkey: meat 'loaf' with olive salsa
    183
Tuscan white bean soup with ham
    & thyme 87

V

Vietnamese beef pho 82
Vietnamese pulled pork summer
    rolls 62–4

W

Waldorf salad with smoked ham &
    buttermilk dressing 102
walnuts
    chocolate orange truffles 199
    lemon & walnut goats' cheese
        blinis with blackberries 55
    lentil, peach & halloumi
        panzanella with walnut
        dressing 111
    Waldorf salad with ham 102
    walnut-stuffed chicory cups with
        artichoke & feta purée 65
watercress
    chestnut, blue cheese &
        watercress 'pizzas' on
        marinated mushrooms 123
    chicken & duck pots with winter
        salad 176–8
    herby soft cheese tart with
        grapes & watercress 118–20
    smoked salmon crêpe cake with
        watercress salad 170
    Waldorf salad with ham 102
watermelon pizza with fig, feta &
    raspberry dressing 124
wheatgerm
    'carrot-cake' overnight oats 35
    ginger power balls 38
    peach melba smoothie bowl 31

Y

yoghurt
    balsamic cherry fool 203
    chicken & duck pots 176–8
    falafel wraps with spinach pesto
        & pickled red cabbage 128–30
    five-spiced duck noodle salad
        with pak choi slaw 108
    fruit sushi with coconut &
        passion fruit dip 29–30
    Greek yoghurt pannacotta 207
    herby soft cheese tart with nutty
        pastry & grapes 118–20
    peach melba smoothie bowl 31
    poppy seed 'pancakes' with
        lemon ricotta yoghurt 26
    raita 187
    smoked mackerel kedgeree 40
    striped smoothie jelly 214–15

GRATITUDE

High-fives to all who have cheered me on since the publication of my first book, *No-bake Baking*. Your unbelievable support and encouragement has enabled and inspired me to write this follow-up. That goes for my family and friends too, you are all awesome.

Slam dunk to my fabulous editor Ione Walder, thanks for punching hard in my corner. It was no easy feat convincing everyone that a cookbook without any cooking was a real thing. Thanks for believing in me and my hare-brained ideas.

A whole cheerleading squad of pom-pom shakes to the rest of Team Quercus for continuing to help make my dreams come true, including Charlotte Fry, Hannah Robinson and all in sales and marketing. An extra-big shake to designers Two Associates, for making the pages look so pretty.

I can't hop, skip and backflip enough for the very talented photographer Cristian Barnett. I know I almost broke you, but I'm glad I could help you discover your inner granny chic. Thanks for your fabulous work.

Triple somersaults for Sarah Watchorn who supported me throughout recipe development, particularly when my hands were tied with baby Poppy. I am so impressed with how you flourished in that time. As for the fruit sushi challenge and 'Mr Crabby' music-maker endurance test, you're welcome. Thanks also for taking heroic charge of the shoot kitchen.

Group hug and pats on the back to the rest of the book shoot team. Sofie Skehan, thanks for your stylish eye, support and gazebo prop chats, which filled me with confidence and kept me sane. Thanks to Joanna Carley for your creative talents, Emma Neary for all your hard work and pleasantness, and Rachel Warren for your great help in digging the trenches.

Endless air-kisses for the girls who added flair to the photos. Joanne Condon at **www.kylelane.ie**, I can't thank you enough for your inspiring backgrounds and props. If only I had an inch of space left in my house to keep that amazing, pimped-up hostess trolley! Thanks also to Claire Ryan and Patsie Wrafter at **www.theinformalflorist.com** and Alana Talbot at **www.project-party.com**.

Big shimmy-shimmy-shakes to all the other fabulous females who give me strength and support. Besides family and friends (you know who you are), I will name a few. Orla Broderick for your enthusiasm for late-night brainstorming. The two Annes who help me keep my life on track, one by rubbing my feet, the other by holding my hand. And supernannies Yvonne and Marion for taking such good care of my babies.

Throw your arms in the air like you just don't care for Donal Skehan, for your fabulous foreword. Thanks for being so encouraging, despite the regular tellings-off for not keeping on top of my social media. Thanks to Rachel Allen and James Martin for very generously supporting the book. A big cheers to all the other chefs in the industry who have taught, inspired and supported me.

Mega air punches to my husband Martin for endless playground trips with the girls while I worked. Plus a long line of cartwheels for once again putting up with the kitchen bombsite and home takeover during testing and shooting.

Finally, skipping ropes at the ready for to my two gorgeous, precious girls who make my heart skip-skip a beat. Thank you Pearl for your honest opinions on which recipes should make it into the book and which definitely shouldn't! What a fab chia-pudding-pop model you made too. Thank you Poppy for being (mostly) a good sleeper while I tended this book by night and for smiling endlessly while I cooked it by day.

Thank you all: I am bursting with gratitude for everyone who helps me climb my mountains.

ABOUT THE AUTHOR

Sharon Hearne-Smith has nearly two decades of experience in ghostwriting, recipe testing and food styling for high-profile cookbooks, food magazines and TV cookery shows. She has worked with some of the biggest names in the business, including Jamie Oliver, Rachel Allen, Lorraine Pascale, Gordon Ramsay, James Martin, and on BBC's *Ready Steady Cook*. Sharon lives in Dublin with her husband and two daughters. Her first cookbook *No-bake Baking* was published by Quercus in 2014. This is her second cookbook.

Quercus Editions Ltd
Carmelite House
50 Victoria Embankment
London EC4Y 0DZ

An Hachette UK Company

First published in 2016

A catalogue record of this book is available from the British Library

ISBN 978 1 78429 712 1

Commissioning editor: Ione Walder
Design: Two Associates
Food styling: Sharon Hearne-Smith
Prop styling: Sofie Larsson & Sharon Hearne-Smith
Copy-editing: Sarah Chatwin

Printed and bound in China

10 9 8 7 6 5 4 3 2 1